S0-AIJ-949

B95
COF/TRN
0827x1

The frigate USS Constitution *acquired the soubriquet "Old Ironsides" because of her stout timber construction and the mettle of her crew. The term "ironclad" applied to ships protected from shot and shell by iron plating, regardless of the material of the underlying construction. The first ironclads were timber ships covered with iron plates; later ships were iron built but the armor was fixed over timber sheathing. Ironclad continued to be used to describe armored ships after the introduction of compound (iron and steel) armor, and then of steel construction. The word fell into disuse about the end of the nineteenth century for ships, but the reputation of the ironclad has left its mark in the language.*

A wader is a water bird that paddles in shallow water, but the word "paddler" was used to describe a ship propelled by paddle wheels—that is to say, all steamships before the introduction of the screw.

Plate 1.

The Black Battle Fleet
in the Tagus off Lisbon, Portugal, 1875

The Black Battle Fleet was a popular term for the Royal Navy's ironclads. They were formidably long ships with all-black hulls and coal-burning means of propulsion. To contemporary eyes ironclads had a sinister aspect in contrast to the familiar three-decker man-of-war, with its towering sides of super-imposed gunports painted in checkerboard fashion.

The Channel Squadron of the British fleet is seen in the River Tagus off the Portuguese capital, Lisbon. Portugal was for centuries England's most consistent European ally, and the relationship had been enhanced by their common cause during the Napoleonic Wars.

In the forefront is HMS *Minotaur* and beyond her lies her sister ship *Agincourt*, both rigged with five masts as they were when first built. Enlargements of the original *Warrior* design, the two ships remained in first-line service for nearly thirty years. Their iron hulls continued to do duty as training ships and then as hulks well into the twentieth century: *Agincourt* was not broken up until 1960.

On the left is the forepart of HMS *Hercules*, beyond her is HMS *Research*, and in the background HMS *Invincible*.

All these ironclads were built in the 1860s. The *Agincourt* class carried a tremendous armament of four nine-inch and twenty-four seven-inch rifles which were mounted behind ports along the five-and-one-half-inch-thick armored sides. *Research* was one of the first with a central battery layout, her four 100-pounder smoothbores being concentrated in an armored "box" and arranged so that they could fire broadside and forward or broadside and aft. The *Hercules* had embrasures to give four of her guns a wider field of fire, and the *Invincible* was one of the *Audacious* class which carried ten nine-inch rifles in a central battery, four of them in upper deck sponsons jutting out of the ships' sides to allow a measure of end-on fire.

Excerpt from *The Price of Admiralty* by John Keegan,
copyright ©1988, Hutchinson. Reprinted by permission of
Random House.

Designed by Carolyn Weary Brandt
Edited by Melissa E. Barranco and Ross A. Howell, Jr.

Text and illustrations copyright ©1993 by Ian Marshall.
All rights reserved.

This book, or any portions thereof, may not be reproduced
or transmitted in any form or by any means, electronic or
mechanical, including photocopying, recording, or by any
information retrieval system, without permission in writing
from the publisher.

Printed and bound in Hong Kong

Published by Howell Press, Inc., 1147 River Road, Suite 2,
Charlottesville, VA 22901, telephone 804-977-4006.

Library of Congress Catalog Card Number 93-79036

ISBN 0-943231-62-0

First printing

HOWELL PRESS

IRONCLADS
AND PADDLERS

PAINTINGS AND TEXT BY IAN MARSHALL
FOREWORD BY JOHN MAXTONE-GRAHAM

CONTENTS

Plate 2.

SMS *Kaiser*
Port Arthur, Manchuria, 1898

The warship's blunt stem, characteristic of a nineteenth century ironclad, is decorated with scrollwork bearing the German Imperial Eagle in place of the traditional figurehead. SMS *Kaiser* was built on the Thames in London as a central-battery ironclad. Her principal armament was mounted in an armored redoubt amidships, jutting out slightly over the tumble home of the ship's sides.

In 1890 the ironclad was reconstructed and given a new rating as an armored cruiser. Ship rig was removed and replaced by two military masts supporting platforms for quick-firers and for observation, and the main armament was supplemented by 5.9-inch guns in modern swivel mountings on the upper deck.

The white-painted armored cruiser was posted for many years in the China seas as part of the German Asiatic Squadron. She served as the flagship of Rear Admiral Alfred von Tirpitz, who was responsible for establishing a naval base at Tsingtao on the China coast.

Tirpitz's successor was Rear Admiral Otto von Diederichs, and it was during his period of command that the *Kaiser* was ordered to Manila with a view to securing the German claim to the ex-Spanish colony of the Philippines.

Commodore George Dewey USN had other views. He had just sunk the Spanish naval force in Manila Bay and his squadron lay off the city pending arrival of sufficient troops to enable the U.S. to take possession of the islands. He insisted on the courtesy of a salute from the German ships. Diederichs, in spite of the superiority of the *Kaiser* and other German warships, was given instructions to withdraw.

ILLUSTRATIONS

Plate 3.

USS *Franklin* and *Richmond*
Villefranche, France, 1871

Admiral David Farragut was given command of the European squadron which was sent to the Mediterranean in 1867 to "show the flag" after the American Civil War. His flagship was the screw frigate USS *Franklin*.

She was laid down in 1854 at Portsmouth, New Hampshire, but completed only in 1867. During the Civil War the most urgent need of the U.S. Navy was for shallow-draft vessels for inshore work rather than for more frigates.

Her displacement was 5,200 tons and she mounted four 100-pounder rifled guns, one eleven-inch smoothbore, and thirty-four nine-inch smoothbores along the sides.

The second ship is the sloop USS *Richmond*, a sister ship of Farragut's flagship at the Battle of Mobile Bay, USS *Hartford*. *Richmond* was commissioned in 1860 and took an active part in the war, being rammed by CSS *Manassas* in 1861, damaged by gunfire at Pensacola and Vicksburg, and engaged by CSS *Webb* at New Orleans. After the war she served in Europe, the West Indies, the South Pacific, China, and the South Atlantic before being retired to training duties in 1890.

Richmond was a screwship armed initially with fourteen nine-inch smoothbores, later to be supplemented by rifled guns mounted on deck.

Villefranche, near Nice, was used as a regular coaling station by the European squadron. Earlier it was used as the Mediterranean base of the Russian Navy, but this privilege was brought to an end when the port passed from Italian to French sovereignty in 1860.

PREFACE

I owe a great debt to scholarly historians, particularly to D. K. Brown, the author of *Before the Ironclad*, and others who worked from original sources. I have depended on the work of diligent researchers and biographers: this book is the celebration of an era, it makes no claim to break new ground.

I wish to pay tribute to the help and encouragement of my incomparable wife Jean, to the proprietors of galleries on both sides of the Atlantic who show my work, Oliver Swann and Frank O'Rourke, and to Agostino von Hassell. The text would have been much clumsier but for the painstaking intervention of Commander Laurence Newman Jr., USN (Ret).

I.H.M., Mount Desert Island, Maine, 1993

This book is dedicated to my brother
Robert
who was in at the beginning.

FOREWORD

To his readers' infinite advantage, Ian Marshall's lifelong passion for battleships is coupled with an extraordinary talent for painting them. The illustrations in this volume are uniquely his, scrupulously accurate, and executed with exactly the kind of heroic grandeur that the subject demands.

Marshall introduced us to battleships in his informative and evocative *Armored Ships* two years ago. Now, in this sequel, the author lays some retroactive groundwork, setting the stage for the capital ships of his first book with a fascinating techno-maritime overture. We are first introduced to fighting paddle steamers, designed originally for use in river warfare. Once these river cruisers were, inevitably, dispatched to deeper contested waters, vulnerable paddles and their protective sponsons were superseded by more efficient underwater screws. With Marshall as our incomparable guide, we follow replacement of planking with plating, topped by an increasingly menacing array of turrets and armor cladding; such were the seesaw offensive/defensive specifications that preoccupied the world's admiralties no less than their naval architects.

Since the author must dwell on the nineteenth century, he deals largely with Great Britain's Royal Navy, a service often dominated, as Marshall informs us, by sea lords who remained hidebound traditionalists. (It is worth remembering that this was the naval establishment that once cautioned, straight-faced, that iron hulls would sink.) Marshall tracks the careers of two outstanding exceptions: Lord Thomas Cochrane, whose derring-do naval career spanned the Napoleonic Wars, and "Jackie" Fisher, who rose to become First Sea Lord by the outbreak of the Great War he had long anticipated. Both of these resourceful, indomitable, and invaluable men belong in these pages for they might well be described as human battleships themselves.

Most of Marshall's towering steel wonders never fired a shot in anger. The few that did engage an enemy fleet often discovered fearsome inadequacies that sent naval planners back to the drawing boards in quest of more powerful armament or additional tons of armor plate. Stationary land-based batteries figure in Marshall's tale as well, for the successful defense of Britain's far-flung island bases was a crucial factor of naval one-upmanship; the author provides capsule histories of Bermuda and Malta, two of the Royal Navy's most memorable island redoubts.

But enough, the fleet is stirring. Aldis lamps clatter and signal flags stream aloft; companionways are unrigged, torpedo booms lashed inboard, and cutters snugged up to their davits. As mud-bedaubed anchors break surface to be hosed clean, funnels gout billows of black smoke. Ian Marshall's splendid, brooding ironclads are bound for sea and we reader/devotees are lucky enough to have been piped on board.

—John Maxtone-Graham
New York City, 1993

Plate 4.

HMS *Iron Duke*
Kowloon, Hong Kong, 1880

Portrayed in a bucolic setting as she undergoes maintenance work in the dry dock at Kowloon, the *Iron Duke* illustrates the widespread role of nineteenth century ironclads.

One of six ships of the *Audacious* class built in the period 1867-1873, *Iron Duke* was intended primarily for service on foreign stations. She had an eight-inch wrought-iron armored belt, tapering to six inches towards the ends of the ship, laid over a backing of ten-inch to eight-inch teak. The main battery carried six nine-inch muzzle-loading rifles firing through broadside ports. The upper battery, which can be seen projecting from the side of the ship, carried four more nine-inch guns in angled ports capable of providing a measure of fore-and-aft fire. Four six-inch rifled guns were mounted at the extreme ends of the upper deck. The ship carried four fourteen-inch torpedoes. *Iron Duke* had twin engines and shafts and was capable of fourteen knots.

The ironclad was commissioned in 1871 and was dispatched to Hong Kong as a flagship in 1871-1875. She was the first capital ship to pass through the recently-opened Suez Canal. *Iron Duke* served again on the China Station in 1878-1883, and was retired in 1900.

Other ships of the same class served in China after the *Iron Duke*, in the Pacific, based in Esquimalt, and in the Mediterranean. They served in home waters as guard ships at Hull, Southampton, Queenstown, Invergordon, Rosyth, and at Kingstown (Dublin).

INTRODUCTION

Emblematic of the worldwide scope of nineteenth century sea power, the ironclad HMS *Iron Duke* lies in dry dock at Kowloon, Hong Kong, in 1880. She and others like her were the ultimate weapon of the day.

Command of the sea had for four centuries been the key to the exploitation of new markets, to the propagation of colonies, and to the growth of national prosperity.

Portugal challenged the commercial monopoly of Venice by pioneering the sea route to India. Naval control of the Indian Ocean protected her profitable mercantile trade and allowed the growth of flourishing trading posts and colonial cities along the coasts of Africa, India, and as far afield as China. Spain contested Portugal's maritime supremacy, and then the Peninsular nations themselves faced competition in turn from Holland, France, and Britain.

Command of the sea enabled the transport of troops and the selective application of military force. At the same time it could deny such freedom of action to a rival power. An unassailable navy not only enabled a small country like Britain to resist the pressure of far stronger nations whose power was restricted to the land, but also exerted a pervasive worldwide influence.

By the early years of the nineteenth century the European man-of-war had evolved through long competition into a type, superbly strong and well adapted to its job. Maritime nations devoted immense resources to the design and construction of these ships, and there was no great difference between those which were built for different navies. British, French, Dutch, and Spanish ships all looked much alike. Such men-of-war carried a concentration of firepower which far exceeded anything that could be mustered on land, and the wooden ships themselves were extraordinarily difficult to sink. A man-of-war embodied the very peak of available technology, highly tuned, effective, and beautiful.

The military historian John Keegan gives this marvelous characterization:

Little wonder that the few survivors of the wooden world—Vasa, Victory, Constitution—command the awed veneration of a later generation. Any great wooden ship, but particularly the wooden man-of-war, is a monument to human ingenuity of a unique sort. Nothing else made by man to coax power from the elements while defying their force has ever so perfectly embodied his intentions. The successors of the wooden man-of-war would go further, shoot further and hit harder than anything wrought from oak, fastened by copper and rigged with flax and hemp; but no product of the shipwright's art—perhaps not even the nuclear submarine—would ever serve the purposes of those who pay and those who command so narrowly.

The traditional wooden line-of-battle ship often had a service life of more than sixty years, and a naval officer's skills, slowly and painfully acquired, long retained their usefulness.

Early in the new century the pace of change began to quicken. Improved structural techniques enabled the building of larger, stronger, and much more powerful wooden ships. Steam power was introduced at first for tugs whose job it was to tow them in and out of harbor, but later it was employed to provide propulsion for the men-of-war themselves. The first use of iron in shipbuilding was for components forming part of the structure of a wooden ship,

HMS Alexandra 1877

and then in the 1820s came the first iron-built ships.

Evolution took place also in the field of gunnery. The carronade had been introduced in the latter years of the eighteenth century, making available greatly increased firepower for smaller ships at short range. The growing power of cannons and the use of explosive projectiles led eventually to the extinction of the wooden man-of-war.

Paddle warships came into naval service in the 1830s, and the invention of screw propulsion accelerated the transition from sail to steam. Conventional wooden square-rigged men-of-war were given steam engines in time to dominate naval strategy in the Crimean War of 1855-1856.

It was, above all, the introduction of armor cladding that brought about the great change. From 1860 onwards there was a revolution in warship design. The first ironclads were nearly unsinkable, and so maritime powers bent their ingenuity to devise bigger guns to penetrate their armor, and in response called forth thicker and stronger armor with which to resist attack.

The concepts of the mine, the torpedo, the torpedo boat, and the submarine all germinated during the course of the nineteenth century, to emerge as practicable weapons towards its close. Each new development was expected to be the nemesis of the armored ship, but by the end of the century it had reached its apogee in terms of numbers and prestige.

To evoke the era of the ironclads it is necessary to do more than portray the ships and describe the evolution of their design. Two people and two places have been chosen to give color to the story.

The professional careers of two famous sailors between them spanned the period. The first was Thomas Cochrane, who entered the Royal Navy in 1793. The story of Lord Cochrane's life reads like an historical novel, and it must surely have been the model which inspired C. S. Forester's endearing fictional character of Admiral Lord Hornblower.

But there was more to Cochrane than panache. The Scotsman became the most dashing and admired frigate captain of his day, but he was also a character of unyielding principle whose path through life became strewn with irritated officials. He played a prominent role as a Radical reformer in Parliament; he fought corruption and unjust practices which were deeply entrenched in the administration of the Royal Navy; and for ten years he went abroad to fight for the cause of fledgling democracies in South America and Greece.

Cochrane inherited from his father an interest in scientific experiment, which led to a predilection for the use of explosive devices and a restless search for improved weapons and new means of propulsion.

His prickly personality and cavalier behavior aroused antagonism which led eventually to trial before the High Court. There he faced trumped-up charges before a dishonest judge, was convicted of fraud, disgraced, and cashiered from the Navy. Even then, however, Cochrane's humanity and gallantry inspired loyalty and admiration, and he lived to vindicate his name, to be reinstated to high honors, and to reach the rank of Admiral of the Fleet. At the age of seventy-nine his appointment as Commander-in-Chief in the Crimean War was considered by the government, but it was denied on the grounds that "this gallant officer might commit the fleet to some desperate enterprise where the chance of success would not countervail the risk of failure."

The name of the second sailor—"Jackie" Fisher—is more familiar. John Fisher started as a midshipman at the time when Admiral Lord Cochrane was in command in the West Indies. As a young man Fisher showed evidence of a stormy and ambitious character, and starting without advantages he gained rapid promotion. He too was fascinated by technological progress, taking an enthusiastic interest in new types of warship, new weapons, and new tactics of naval warfare. His meteoric career was aided by an impish charm that secured him access to the great and the good. Like Cochrane, Fisher was a crusader for reform, impatiently sweeping aside crusty individuals and conservative practices. His sharp intelligence and the fury of his energy transformed a navy that was married to traditional ways.

This nineteenth-century excursion concludes with a visit to two of the island bases that sustained the Black Battle Fleet[1] in its worldwide operations. Bermuda and Malta were both intimately associated with the careers of the two admirals.

---

[1] Wooden line-of-battle ships had more than one gundeck and were painted in alternate strakes of black and white or ochre. Ironclads were long and low, and they were painted in unrelieved black. Hence this popular term.

Plate 5.

USS *Scorpion*, *Spitfire*, *Scourge*, and *Bonita*

on the Tabasco River, Mexico, 1847

During the Mexican War which followed the U.S. annexation of Texas, the U.S. Navy Home Squadron under Commodore Matthew Perry landed 12,000 men at Vera Cruz and captured every port from Yucatán to Tampico. Four side-wheel paddle steamers were purchased for service with the Navy, and three of them together with the schooner

USS *Bonita* took part in the expedition up the Tabasco River.

The steamers, under the command of Commander Bigelow, were employed in towing forty ships' boats full of troops to make landings in the mesquite, and in supporting the assault on the city of Tabasco.

Paddlers had advantages over screw-powered vessels for operating in very shallow water; they were more maneuverable and they could proceed with equal ease forwards or backwards. During the American Civil War paddle steamers played the leading role in river campaigns.

EVOLUTION OF THE IRONCLAD

The story of the evolution in warship design from sail to steam, the switch from paddlers to screw propulsion, early experiments with iron construction, and, finally, the introduction of the armored ship is a tangled one. Developments took place not so much in sequence as in several fields simultaneously. There were false starts, ideas that proved beyond the means of available industrial resources, and occasional reversions to the old ways.

It would be wrong to portray the process as a sequence of brilliant innovations, still less as the story of a hidebound service reluctant to adapt to change. What seems in hindsight to have been the obvious way forward was by no means the case at the time.

An iron hull, for example, would play the devil with a magnetic compass. The use of iron to build oceangoing vessels had to await the solution to this problem. A technique was eventually found for placing pieces of iron around the compass in order to counteract the magnetic effects of the hull, after which the ship would be "swung" around its mooring in order to make all the necessary corrections.

In the first half of the nineteenth century there was continuing progress in the technology of wood construction. This led to the building of larger, stronger, and faster ships. Right up to the 1860s the wooden three-decker ship-of-the-line, with its overwhelming concentration of firepower, continued to be the unrivaled master of the situation.

Steam power, introduced at the beginning of the century, took 100 years to displace sail entirely. Sailing ships were still in widespread commercial use up to 1914.

Early steam engines were so uneconomical that their application was limited to situations where passage under sail was difficult, such as on inland waterways. Steamers came in first with paddles, and it was not until the adoption of screw propulsion that steam power became good for general use in warships. The proposition of discarding sailing rig entirely had to await the duplication of engines in order to offset their lack of reliability.

Iron construction offered improved strength for weight, durability, and incombustibility, but the material proved shockingly liable to shatter under the impact of shot. Early expectations of iron's resistance to cannon fire were dashed in tests, and the use of armor cladding was delayed until the introduction of composite systems. Indeed it was still the practice to fix steel armor over a backing of teak when the battleship *Bismarck* was built in 1940.

The story is predominantly a British one. The whole nation recognized that survival in the Napoleonic Wars had depended on command of the sea. Throughout the nineteenth century Britain was the leading trading nation, and British ships comprised the lion's share of worldwide seafaring traffic. Britain and India accounted for ten percent and eighteen percent of the world's manufacturing output in 1830, and with the growth of free trade Britain became more and more dependent on overseas commerce, for export as well as for the import of food and raw materi-

HMS *Caledonia* 1865

als. In 1857 the Indian Mutiny emphasized the vital importance of uninterrupted sea communications.

No wonder that the island nation maintained a navy always superior to any combination of forces which seemed likely to be formed against her. In the last resort the security of the British Empire rested on the battle fleet, and from 1865 this was composed of not more than a score of ironclads.

Admiral Lord Fisher, the most important figure in nineteenth century naval history, emphasized the suddenness and finality of sea battle. In the case of a great naval battle, he said, all would be decided in a few hours. "Once beaten, the war is finished. Beaten on land, you can

improvise fresh armies in a few weeks. You can't improvise a fresh Navy; it takes four years."

His point was proven in 1905. On the afternoon of May 29th the Russian fleet was destroyed by the Japanese. Defeat in the Battle of Tsushima cost Russia the war.

Improvements in Wood Construction

After 1815 warship design evolved initially in the field of improved structural techniques. Britain had experienced a shortage of building materials: large fir trees for masts were less readily available from America, and there was a crisis in the supply of seasoned oak from homegrown sources in the last years of the Napoleonic Wars.

Legend has it that Admiral Lord Nelson, on his last visit to England before his death at the Battle of Trafalgar, was asked to visit the woodcutters in the Forest of Dean. Encouraging the workmen, he observed the shortage of new growth and gave orders for fresh plantations. These trees were in their prime 130 years later, when the Admiralty in 1935, seeing no further use for them, ordered the oaks to be felled. In 1940 German magnetic mines posed an unprecedented threat to ships with steel hulls, and Nelson's oak came in handy for the construction of wooden minesweepers.

Back in 1813 Sir Robert Seppings was appointed Chief Constructor of the Royal Navy. He devoted his attention to structural methods to enable the construction of larger ships with longer gundecks. He was also concerned to make better use of the smaller sizes of timber which were more readily available. He introduced diagonal bracing within the main framing, iron knees in place of naturally grown timber ones which were especially hard to get, continuous shelf construction to support the deck beams, and diagonal deck planking. Masts were built up from multiple small elements and a number of ships were constructed in Bombay using teak instead of English oak.

The traditional hull form was modified at bow and stern to give greater structural strength and protection against enemy shot. In the process of rounding both extremities provision was made for gunports capable of providing a measure of fore and aft fire.

Under Sir William Symonds, Seppings' successor with the title of Surveyor, the wooden line-of-battle ship gained further size and speed. No longer was it possible for an enemy to depend on being able to flee from the world's strongest battle fleet. Broader gundecks and wider spacing of guns enabled the arming of the battle fleet with guns of a single caliber. Instead of superimposed batteries of 32-, 24-, and 18-pounders, all three gundecks now carried 32-pounder weapons of uniform range and power. Improved techniques of gun casting, finer tolerances between shot and bore, and attention to the education and training of the crew led to greatly improved accuracy and rate of fire.

The last of the great wooden liners, built in the 1850s, had twice the displacement of Nelson's *Victory*, and they fired double her weight of shot and shell. The effectiveness of their gunpower was multiplied by a factor of rather more than two.

It would be a mistake to visualize the wooden battle fleet being gradually rendered ineffectual through the evolution of new forms of weapon, propulsion, and construction. On the contrary, the liner was made steadily more powerful. From 1846 each large warship in the Royal Navy would be accompanied by a steamer capable of towing her, of defending her against other steamers, and of pursuing a fleeing enemy in a calm. Professional opinion rated the three-decker indispensable in the ultimate confrontation between naval powers, and this judgment stimulated the effort to equip the battle fleet with screw propulsion rather than replace it with small steamers armed with swivel-mounted guns.

Steam Power

A ship under sail needs sea room. Square-riggers cannot sail close to the wind, and they would find themselves trapped for days in harbor waiting for a change in the weather. A sailing ship is least effective when attempting to navigate in canals and narrow rivers.

It was in inland waterways, therefore, that steam power first became useful. Steamers were employed as tugs to bring oceangoing ships in and out of harbor regardless of the direction of the wind.

Early steam engines were inefficient, they were extravagant in fuel, and they were heavy and bulky by later standards. The use of steam was therefore constrained to situations where sail power was least efficient. Long passages under steam were prohibitively expensive, and there were very few places in the world where one could find stocks of coal for bunkering.

The first regular use was made of steam propulsion as

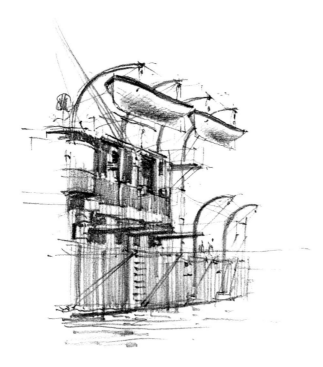

far back as 1802. The paddler *Charlotte Dundas* was employed for towing barges on the Forth and Clyde Canal. Fulton's and Livingston's *Clermont* started plying the Hudson River in 1807, and a few years later Bell's *Comet* started beating up and down the Clyde. Soon the Mississippi, the Ohio, and—after 1825—the waters of the Erie Canal were being churned by stern-wheelers, and a side-wheeler was pressed into use as a transport at the Battle of New Orleans in the War of 1812.

The U.S. Navy ordered construction of a steam-powered battery to be used in the defense of New York, but fighting came to an end before this ship, the *Demologos*, entered naval service. She had a single paddle wheel operating in a slot on the centerline of the hull and she was to have mounted twenty-four guns.

Serious strides were made in steam navigation during the 1820s and 1830s. The first passage from England to Calcutta under steam was accomplished by a 500-ton paddler named *Enterprise* in 1825, and in 1838 the little *Sirius*—just barely—became the first to steam across the Atlantic. She had to burn her cabin furniture to achieve that distinction, but Isambard Brunel's *Great Western*, which arrived a few hours later with coal in hand, went on

to make regular and profitable crossings.

The Admiralty ordered several steamships in 1821, mainly for use as tugs. Most readers will be familiar with J.M.W. Turner's opulent sunset painting entitled "The Fighting *Téméraire* tugged to her last berth." It was painted in 1839.

The U.S. Navy used a steamship in the Caribbean in 1822, and the fledgling Greek Navy employed three paddle warships in the War of Independence, 1827.

It should be no cause for surprise that the East India Company was a pioneer of steam navigation. As the world's largest trading enterprise it had a burning interest in faster and more reliable means of communication. Just as the Mississippi, the Great Lakes, and the Erie Canal gave access to the heartland of America, so the Ganges and the Indus provided strategic and trade connections to a vast and populous hinterland.

The sea route from the subcontinent to Europe around the Cape of Good Hope was enormously extended, and the Company concentrated on developing direct overland links between the Persian Gulf or the Red Sea and the eastern Mediterranean. The early use of steam packets across the English Channel and the Mediterranean was soon followed by a regular steamer service from Bombay to Suez. This route was inaugurated in 1837.

The Royal Navy commissioned its first steam-powered fighting ship in 1836. This vessel, HMS *Gorgon*, had a displacement of 1,100 tons, a speed of ten knots, and an armament of sixteen 42-pounder and 68-pounder guns. She played a prominent part in the Syrian campaign of 1840 and later in operations up the River Plate and the Parana in South America.

Gorgon was the prototype of a whole generation of paddlers in naval service. The great value of these craft was their ability to work in shallow waters, close inshore or upriver, where maneuverability in the face of current or tide was of overriding importance. It was this capability that enabled maritime power to be projected for the first time far inland. Armed detachments were landed with the support of naval gunfire hundreds of miles up the Irrawaddy in

Plate 6.

HEICoS *Nemesis*
on the Irrawaddy River, Burma, 1852

The world's first iron fighting ship was delivered to the East India Company in 1840.

Paddlers had been in naval use for twenty years as tugs, and for offensive operations in restricted waters where sailing ships lacked the space to maneuver. The East India Company was a pioneer in the use of iron-hulled vessels, which had advantages over wooden ones, particularly for navigation in shallow rivers. It was in 1835 that the company took the step of ordering an iron "war steamer" from Lairds of Birkenhead. This ship, the *Nemesis*, made the passage to India around the Cape of Good Hope in 1840.

Nemesis and her sister ships were a striking success. Her first mission was in China, where her shallow draught enabled her to circumvent the principal river defenses below Canton, and her armament of two 32-pounders swivel-mounted on deck, supplemented by rockets, proved extremely effective in destroying forts as well as armed junks.

Nemesis carried out long service for the East India Company, including operations in Borneo, India, and the Persian Gulf. She took part in the First and Second Burma Wars, leading an expedition 250 miles up the Irrawaddy River to Prome.

Plate 7.

HMS *Jackall*
on the Benue River, Nigeria, 1854

Iron-built shallow-draught gunboats were the first warships capable of penetrating inland up the great rivers of Asia and Africa.

Jackall, which was built on the Clyde in 1844, served in the Navy for more than forty years. Much of her career was spent in West Africa, where she was employed on anti-slavery duties and in the suppression of piracy. She is pictured here on the River Benue, the principal tributary of the Niger, which joins the mainstream some 250 miles from the sea.

In the foreground is the veranda of the District Commissioner's bungalow. He can be seen on the jetty, with officers who are returning to the gunboat.

Burma, the Nile, the Euphrates, and the Niger. The Yangtze-Kiang in China is navigable for an incredible 1,400 miles upriver from its mouth in the Yellow Sea. Steamers, operating in conjunction with ships-of-the-line, were able to penetrate into the heart of the Chinese Empire and to impose conditions enabling the opening of Chinese ports to European trade.

During the Mexican War of 1846-1848 four side-wheel paddle steamers were taken into service by the U.S. Navy. These ships, *Scorpion*, *Spitfire*, *Vixen*, and *Scourge*, towed landing craft and supported the troops once they were ashore at Vera Cruz, in the Tabasco River, and at other points along the Gulf Coast. The flagship of Commodore Matthew Perry's squadron which was sent to overawe Japan into granting America trading access in 1854 was a side-wheel paddler called USS *Powhatan*.

Paddle steamers, most of them converted from civilian use, played a big role in the river campaigns of the American Civil War. The last paddle frigate in the Royal Navy was not removed from the navy list until 1891.

But for naval purposes paddlers had serious drawbacks. The paddle wheels themselves presented a vulnerable target, and they occupied a large part of the side of the ship, preempting space which would otherwise be available for the battery. Perhaps most importantly, the paddles were much affected by the degree of immersion: if the ship was laden and lay deep in the water their efficiency was impaired, and the same was true if the ship rode too high. In rough weather the paddles would be alternately immersed and left flailing in the air, and they tended to suffer damage from heavy seas. The paddles could be disconnected, or the floats could be feathered when not in use, but even so operating a paddle ship under sail presented difficulties.

The paddle was phased out in favor of the screw for warships, but the special attributes of paddlers continued to be useful in certain situations. In very shallow water, where shifting mudbanks make grounding a not infrequent experience, there is a lot to be said for a paddleboat. The maneuverability of a side-wheeler is phenomenal: with one wheel stationary, or even thrown into reverse, the ship can

be swivelled on a dime. For many years screw-ships were plagued by vibration which was beyond the power of engineers to subdue.

So paddle steamers continued to be built for use on the Hudson, the Ganges, and the Congo. Queen Victoria's steam yacht *Victoria and Albert* proceeded with a stately, rhythmic beat, and so did the tiny *Alberta*, on which the queen made her last journey from the Isle of Wight to Portsmouth in 1901. Paddle tugs were constructed for the Royal Navy as recently as the 1950s.

The most surprising reappearance of the paddler occurred when the U.S. Navy commissioned two wooden side-wheelers, *Sable* and *Wolverine*, as aircraft carriers for training purposes on Lake Michigan during the Second World War.

Today you can still take a paddler down the River Clyde, and each year two stern-wheelers still indulge in a race up the Mississippi.

Screw Propulsion

Two men, working independently, managed to devise workable methods of screw propulsion. One was John Ericsson, a Swede, and the other was an Englishman, Francis Petit Smith, both of whom were granted patents in London in 1836.

Ericsson's experimental screw-powered launch *Francis B. Ogden* was demonstrated to the Admiralty in 1837. The admirals were not impressed. It may be that his personality, which has been described as eccentric and imperious, had something to do with Ericsson's reception.

Smith showed his boat, *Francis Smith*, to the admirals six months later. He was instructed to produce a larger ship for experiment, and this vessel, called *Archimedes*, was used for trials in competition with paddlers across the English Channel in 1838.

The screw-propelled *Archimedes* caught the attention of the great engineer Isambard K. Brunel when the vessel visited Bristol, and he leased her to carry out trials of his own. As a result of these tests the design of his second transatlantic passenger steamship *Great Britain* was changed in 1840 from paddle to screw propulsion. There were still large areas of uncertainty about the optimum size and type of screw propellers and the best way to mount them in the hull, but Brunel's intuitive sense seems to have got it largely right. Recent tests of Brunel's design showed that its performance compares quite well with modern propellers.

Ericsson found a patron in the U.S. consul in Liverpool, Captain Robert Stockton, USN. The Swedish engineer transferred his work to New York, where his ideas were readily accepted and a number of merchant ships were fitted with screws to his design. He also made a good impression on the U.S. Navy, and in 1841 construction began on the sloop USS *Princeton*, the world's first screw-propelled man-of-war.

At this stage in its development it was not yet obvious that screw propulsion was more efficient than paddles, but for naval purposes it had a clear advantage. It enabled the entire propulsion system to be put well below the waterline, safe from enemy fire.

The Royal Navy conducted a thorough program of tests. The object was to appraise all aspects of the performance of a screw-ship, under sail and under different conditions of the sea.

The Navy called in Brunel to help advise, and the test program included the construction of two ships of similar power and dimensions, one paddler and one screw-propelled. The most memorable part of the trials—and one that is illustrated in almost every book on the subject—was the tug-of-war between the two vessels, *Rattler* and *Alecto*. This famous contest took place in 1845.

The screw-ship won. Actually the trials as a whole showed no dramatic engineering advantage, but by this time the Navy seems to have been convinced anyway that the future lay with the screw.

The switch to steam power was accelerated by demands for coast defense. There was a popular scare at the prospect of an invasion force being landed stealthily on the undefended English coastline. A French army transported

in steamships, it was suggested, could seize an opportunity when contrary winds prevented intervention by the Navy.

A commission of inquiry made recommendations for the construction of new coastal fortifications, particularly in the vicinity of the country's three principal naval dock-yards. These works were put in hand, and so was one of the commission's other recommendations. This called for steam-powered floating batteries for coast defense.

The proposal was to convert some fourteen men-of-war, frigates, and line-of-battle ships into steamers. They were to be equipped with engines of minimum power, sufficient only to enable them to move into position regardless of the wind in order to intercept an invasion force. The ships were described as blockships, and the first four were ready by 1846.

Screw-powered frigates were laid down for both the French and the British navies in 1844, followed by the conversion of the first line-of-battle ships to screw. By the outbreak of the Crimean War in 1854, the Royal Navy had eighteen steam liners and eight frigates in commission, and the French about half these numbers.

There were many who never believed in the reality of the threat of steam invasion. The Royal Navy kept sailing fleets at both ends of the Channel, capable of making an interception in almost all conditions of wind, and the numbers of French steamers never looked equal to the task.

The Royal Navy's defensive strategy included offensive action against the invasion ports. The most prominent of these was the fortified anchorage of Cherbourg. Screw-powered men-of-war, specialized vessels for coastal operations, were developed for such an assault. Harbors were built at Dover and at Alderney in the Channel Islands to facilitate such counterattacks.

Screw propulsion enhanced the effectiveness of a blockading force as much as it improved the opportunities for invasion. The invention of screw-powered liners simply confirmed the Royal Navy's command of the coasts of the English Channel, and indeed of any other littoral where it chose to deploy the battle fleet.

Plate 8.

USS *Powhatan*
near Yokohama, Japan, 1854

The frigate *Powhatan* was one of a squadron of eight U.S. warships under the command of Commodore Matthew Perry that was sent to Japan to help negotiate a treaty enabling trade to be opened up between the two countries.

She was built at Norfolk, Virginia, between 1847 and 1852 and had a displacement of 3,700 tons. The last side-wheel frigate built for the U.S. Navy, her twin engines and paddles propelled her at eleven knots. Her armament included three eight-inch smoothbores, six 32-pounder rifled muzzle-loaders, and smaller weapons.

Powhatan served as flagship of the East India Squadron 1853-1856 and saw action in the Civil War, being present at the blockade of Mobile, Alabama, and in the two attacks on Fort Fisher, North Carolina. She remained in commission until 1886.

There is a fine model of her in the U.S. Navy Museum at Washington, D.C.

Experience in the Crimean War would show that sailing men-of-war declined to face those equipped with means of propulsion: the screw-powered liners dominated the scene. It also became evident in the Baltic operations that paddlers were invaluable for scouting and for hauling the big ships into position for shore bombardment.

Explosive Shells and Iron Construction

In 1822 General Henri Paixhans, a French artillery officer, published a paper advocating the adoption of small, steam-powered ships armed with guns firing explosive shells. His thesis was that France was at last presented with a tool with which to overturn Britain's dominance at sea, with her superior fleet of wooden square-rigged ships and their legend of invincibility.

Paixhans held that quite small steamers should be able to close up to within decisive range of a man-of-war, especially one which was becalmed. With a single large-caliber gun mounted on deck the steamer could destroy it by firing explosive shells into the towering bulk of the wooden liner.

The prospects of revanche were never quite so attractive as they were painted. A square-rigger, even in a calm, was not that helpless. Explosive shells fired from smoothbore cannon were notoriously inaccurate, because loosely packed powder within the shell and the eccentricity of its fuse caused an erratic flight. Furthermore, shells did not have the range of solid shot.

Nevertheless Paixhans' proposals became official policy in 1837, and by 1840 the French Navy had put together a force of sixteen paddle warships. In the same year the Royal Navy was operating nearly fifty.

The use of explosive shells was not entirely new. Bombs had long been used in mortars employed in siege warfare. The British also employed Congreve rockets with explosive warheads, but they had been unable to solve the problem of accuracy. The missiles were notorious for their erratic behavior in flight and had even been known to return to the sender.

Solid cast-iron shot used by eighteenth century cannon could cripple a ship's sailing abilities and cause terrible casualties amongst the crew, but seldom did they sink a ship in action. As a rule the worst experience was to be dismasted: helpless, a ship in this condition generally surrendered to the enemy. The most dreadful danger was fire: fire leading to explosion of the powder magazine was the ultimate disaster. For this reason it was only with the greatest reluctance that naval officers accepted the risks of taking explosive projectiles on board or of employing red-hot shot in a wooden ship.

The destructive potential of explosive shells became gradually more evident. Tests by the French Navy in 1824 showed how effective they could be against wooden ships. By 1840 the normal "fit" for a first-rate man-of-war was sixty percent solid shot, forty percent explosive shells.

Perception of the threat of fire to wooden ships led to an acute interest in iron construction. Once again the Admiralty followed closely the pioneering work sponsored by the nabobs of the East India Company.

Shipowners learned that barges built of iron were lighter for a given capacity then those built of wood and therefore offered economies in operation. A great commercial enterprise like the East India Company found advantages in the use of iron hulls for barges, and also for its shallow-draft steamers on the Hooghly, the Ganges, and the Indus. Iron-built paddlers operated by the Company in Bengal in the 1830s were 120 feet long but had a draft of as little as two feet.

Iron construction brought with it new difficulties as well as economies. Barnacles and other marine growth accumulate on iron bottoms much more rapidly than on copper-sheathed timber, particularly in tropical seas. The problem does not occur in fresh water.

Another drawback was the electrolytic action between iron and other metals in seawater. Only experience showed how this could be avoided by careful design and construction. More serious was the effect of iron on the magnetic compass which has been mentioned earlier. The

Plate 9.

Mahroussa
Suez Canal, Egypt, 1869

At 8:00 A.M. on 18 November 1869, the Suez Canal was opened by a procession that passed through from the Mediterranean to the Red Sea. The line of ships was headed by the French Imperial Yacht *L'Aigle* carrying the Empress Eugénie, whose cousin Ferdinand de Lesseps was the creator of the canal.

Second ship through was the steam yacht of Ismail Pacha, Khedive of Egypt, which was called *Mahroussa*. The third ship in the procession was the Austro-Hungarian Imperial Yacht *Fantasie* with Emperor Franz Joseph on board.

Astonishingly, the Khedive's yacht is still in service. Renamed *El Horria*, she is maintained in top condition as the Presidential Yacht and is regularly used by President Hosni Mubarak. She can be seen, amongst other ships of the Egyptian Navy, moored within the mole at Alexandria.

Mahroussa was built of iron by Samuda Bros. at Poplar on the Thames in 1865. Originally a side-wheel paddler, she was sent to Glasgow in 1905 to be re-engined by A & J Inglis with new-fangled steam turbines driving triple screws.

Mahroussa was used frequently by King Farouk, including many visits to Monte Carlo, and when he was forced to abdicate by Colonel Gamal Nasser in 1955 she carried the King to exile in Naples.

Plate 10.

HMY *Alberta*
Cowes, Isle of Wight, 1901

Queen Victoria died on 22 January 1901 at Osborne House on the Isle of Wight. A few days later her coffin was conveyed to Portsmouth, on the first part of its journey to Westminster and thence to Windsor, on board HMY *Alberta*. This, the smaller of the Royal yachts, was normally used for crossings to the island because of her ability to come right alongside Trinity Pier in East Cowes.

The new King, Edward VII, and visiting heads of state followed in the principal Royal Yacht, the *Victoria and Albert*, which can be seen waiting in the background.

Also present on this occasion were the German Imperial Yacht *Hohenzollern* and the French fleet flagship, the battle-ship *Masséna*. The Admiralty yacht *Enchantress* and the Royal Yacht *Osborne* took part in the procession following *Alberta*.

In the distance can be seen smoke from warships of the Channel Squadron assembling at Spithead to salute the dead Queen on her last journey across these familiar waters.

One of the eight torpedo-boat destroyers which formed an escort to *Alberta* can be seen on the left of the picture, and in the foreground are the roofs and chimneys of the Royal Yacht Squadron clubhouse.

Flag etiquette is noteworthy. The Royal Standard is worn at half-mast in *Alberta*, and at the mainmast peak in *Victoria and Albert* to denote the presence of the new sovereign. All other flags and ensigns are half-masted in mourning.

Astronomer Royal, Sir George Airy, was called in to investigate this effect and in 1839 he published a paper which demonstrated the principles of the solution. The technique is tedious, but gradually it was adopted for general use.

On the positive side iron hulls proved themselves to be tough and resilient under the effect of running aground. One of the most important structural advantages was the feasibility of creating watertight subdivision by means of bulkheads (subdivision in wood construction is ineffective, due to the yield of the material under changing conditions).

Iron-built ships did not suffer from hogging (drooping of bow and stern) or sagging (drooping of central portion of hull), they needed less maintenance than wooden ones, and they had a long life. There are several instances of iron ships surviving for a hundred years. For example the *Mahroussa*, built on the Thames in 1865, is still in service as Egypt's Presidential Yacht. She was present at the opening of the Suez Canal in 1869 and crossed the Atlantic in 1976 to attend the Bicentennial celebrations in New York. She is kept in spanking new condition at Alexandria.

The East India Company took delivery of its first iron steamship in 1831 and four years later, impressed with its experience with iron steamers, it placed an order for the world's first iron fighting ship.

HEICoS *Nemesis*, like all the Company's iron steamers, was built by Lairds of Birkenhead. She had a displacement of 660 tons and a draft of six feet, her hull was divided into seven watertight compartments, and she carried two swivel-mounted 32-pounders on deck plus smaller guns and a rocket launcher.

Nemesis made the passage to India in 1840. A crack which developed in the hull nearly caused the loss of the ship in the Indian Ocean, but she was repaired and had a long and active service life. She took part in the Opium War in China (1841-1843), her shallow draft enabling her to reach Canton by evading the main channel of the Whampoa River which was well defended by forts. She did great destruction amongst war junks and land defenses, and

in one engagement she was struck by fourteen shot without suffering serious damage. *Nemesis* and the iron-built *Phlegethon*, together with other Company steamers, also took part in the First and Second Burma Wars (1852-1853) and in operations against pirates on the northwest coast of Borneo.

The publication of Airy's work on the correction of compasses precipitated Brunel's decision to change the design of SS *Great Britain* from wood to iron construction. With a displacement of 3,670 tons she was by far the largest iron vessel up to that time. Her keel was laid in a specially built dry dock at Bristol in 1839; she was completed five years later and entered service as a passenger liner with a capacity for 250 people.

Great Britain was full of innovations, but her size exceeded the limitations of available technology. She had a checkered career in commercial service, ending it as a sailing craft carrying bulk cargoes. In 1885 she was damaged while rounding Cape Horn and was abandoned in the Falkland Islands. From there she was rescued in 1970 and returned to Bristol, to be installed as a museum ship in the very dry dock in which she had been built. Today one can see the whole underwater sweep of *Great Britain*'s graceful hull, 320 feet long, an impressive monument to the iron industry of 1840.[1]

In 1840 the Admiralty ordered three iron gunboats from Lairds for use on the rivers of West Africa. The shipyard also supplied a 900-ton iron warship called the *Guadaloupe* to Mexico. She proved her worth in the expedition against Yucatán in 1841, and when she withstood the fire of the corvette *Austin* in the Texan War of Independence, 1843.

Growing confidence in the virtues of iron construction led to a decision by the Royal Navy to place orders for five iron frigates of more than 2,000 tons. They were designed to mount from twelve to fourteen guns, some of them 68-pounders. At the same time an experimental program was put in hand to test the effects of cannon shot on an iron hull.

Two series of tests were undertaken, first at

Plate 11.

HMS _Warrior_
steaming out of Devonport, 1861

In 1861 the first iron-built armored warship was put into service by the Royal Navy. She was called the _Warrior_, and her armor was capable of resisting the gunfire of any foreign warship.

She was built to catch and destroy French ironclads and her guns were 68-pounders, twice the size of the standard gun in a ship-of-the-line.

Warrior was designed to carry forty such smoothbore cannon, but before completion some of them were replaced by ten seven-inch breech-loading rifled guns firing 110-pound shot or shell. The breech-loaders proved unreliable and within three years they were all replaced by a mixture of seven-inch and eight-inch rifled muzzle-loaders. Solid steel shot from these weapons could penetrate any armor available up to 1870.

At sea she would normally rely on sail power, for the early engines and boilers were grossly uneconomical as well as unreliable. Her Penn single-expansion horizontal trunk engine could drive her at fourteen knots, but she once made 17.5 knots under sail and steam combined. Her propeller could be hoisted out of the water into the stern, and her funnels were telescopic.

Warrior is passing the Royal William victualing yard as she follows a three-decker out of the Hamoaze and into Plymouth Sound.

Woolwich Arsenal and later at the naval gunnery school on HMS *Excellent*, moored in Portsmouth Harbour. Part of the tests involved firing at a small iron-built launch called HMS *Ruby*. The results were, literally, shattering. The target suffered severely from heavy guns at battle range, sending off a whirlwind of lethal shards which would have caused dreadful casualties within the ship. The ragged holes remaining in half-inch-thick iron plating proved impossible to repair with the usual wooden plugs.

The report of conclusions was extremely adverse to iron construction. Further experiments undertaken between 1846 and 1850 against targets, including iron plates bolted onto timber hulls, delayed further progress towards the use of iron until the end of the decade; the five iron frigates ordered in 1843 were converted to troopships.

New impetus to the idea of iron construction for warships was given by the Battle of Sinope in 1853. In that year Russia went to war with the Ottoman Empire, largely in order to gain accessibility through the Bosphorus and the Straits of Dardanelles to the Mediterranean. Fighting took place on land near the mouth of the Danube in what is now Romania. An overwhelmingly stronger Russian fleet consisting of six liners, three frigates, and two steamers descended on a Turkish squadron anchored near the shore. The Turks comprised six frigates, three corvettes, and two paddlers, none of which mounted guns larger than 24-pounders. The Russian line-of-battle ships included in their armament thirty-eight 60-pounder shell-firing guns. In the course of four hours' bombardment all the Turkish ships were set on fire and burned to the waterline. The Turks suffered 3,000 casualties, three quarters of the crews.

The shock of this disaster drew widespread attention. Most observers took the view that it was explosive shells that were responsible, and that this battle spelled the doom of the wooden man-of-war.

The British government was alarmed at the prospect of Russia dismembering the Ottoman Empire and establishing a fleet with its base in the Mediterranean. The British were always sensitive to any change which might endanger the overland route to India or, after 1869, threaten the Suez Canal. Four times during the course of the century the Navy was sent in to protect the integrity of Turkey.

In 1854-1856 Britain and France together went to war with Russia to stop what looked like her imminent occupation of the Balkan Peninsula. The war was fought in the Baltic as well as in the Black Sea, but the principal military operation was an allied landing in the Crimea with the intention of capturing the naval base at Sevastopol. This was eventually achieved, and the conflict has become known as the Crimean War.

The Ironclad

One outcome of the burning of Turkish ships at the Battle of Sinope was an order by the Emperor of France, Napoleon III, for the construction of ten small armored gunboats called "batteries." Various designs for armor were considered, including fixing boxes of cannonballs along the side of the vessels, but it was decided to go for iron cladding four and one-half inches thick.

Since France had joined Britain to come to the aid of the Turks, the French sought British help in manufacturing the armored ships. It was decided to build five of them in each country.

Three of the French batteries went into action against the forts at Kinburn in 1855.[2] The armored batteries were only a small part of the assault force, which included seventy ships, but their immunity to cannon fire at a range of under 1,000 yards deeply impressed the allies, and caused the Russian commander to surrender in despair.

The Admiralty, it seems, was still cautious after its earlier experience with ships built of iron. It was decided first to conduct further firing tests against armor before embarking on construction. The British armored batteries joined the fleet, therefore, too late to see action, but three more ships were added to the program. These were constructed entirely of iron. One of these iron batteries, HMS *Terror*, served until 1903 as a guard ship at Bermuda.

Next step in the ironclad evolution was the appointment of Dupuy de Lôme as Directeur du Matériel of the French Navy. He endorsed General Paixhans' thesis and, following his own studies of iron construction in England, he pushed forward a bold program to create a steam-powered ironclad navy.

La Gloire was the first product of the new policy. She was a 5,200-ton wooden screw frigate with four-and-three-quarter-inch-thick iron plating over the whole length of the hull. It had been intended to build the entire ship of iron, but the industrial resources of the country were not equal to the task. She was completed in 1860.

News of this development caused a vigorous reaction across the English Channel. Iron construction was enormously costly, and many people had misgivings about starting on a route which could lead to the obsolescence of all existing ships. The Admiralty saw no option but to proceed, and the wealth of the country, coupled with its great lead in production of coal and iron, gave Britain a growing advantage over France in the era of the ironclads.

The Chief Constructor of the Royal Navy, Isaac Watts, had continued the tests on ironclad batteries, iron-built and wooden. He elected to go for iron construction, the main part of the hull being sheathed in eighteen-inch-thick teak, then clad with four-and-one-half-inch-thick iron plates, the joints of which were tongued and grooved. French artillery lacked the punch to penetrate such construction. The ship he designed, HMS *Warrior*, was completed a year later than *La Gloire*. By an extraordinary series of circumstances she has survived to this day. She can be visited in Portsmouth, where she has been restored to her original appearance of 1861. She lies within the Naval Dockyard, not far from the world's only remaining ship-of-the-line, Nelson's flagship HMS *Victory*.

Warrior is a large ship—420 feet long compared with *Victory*'s 186 feet—and her displacement is 9,180 tons. Her hull form is in elegant contrast to the burly shape of the wooden liner. Her two-cylinder Penn trunk engine and single screw drove the ironclad at fourteen knots. The screw could be hoisted out of the water into the stern in order to eliminate its drag while under sail, and the funnels were

telescopic. She carried full square sail rig.

Warrior's armament was all carried on a single gundeck, as in a frigate, with the exception of two pivot guns mounted on the weather deck at bow and stern. She was designed to tackle French ironclads, so her cannon were the biggest available, 68-pounders. She was to have mounted forty of these smoothbore cannon.

This armament was varied twice, once before the ship was completed when breechloaders were substituted. They proved disappointing in performance, and she ended up with muzzle-loading rifled guns, thirty-two of them of seven-inch and eight-inch caliber (110-pounder). It was well within their ability to penetrate the armor of *La Gloire*.

The gunports were spaced widely apart to preserve the strength of the armored side, and the ship appeared to contemporary eyes long and low in the water. Lord Palmerston, seeing her lying amongst the towering three-decker ships-of-the-line with their strakes of black and ochre, described *Warrior* as "a snake amongst the rabbits."

The ironclad was brimming with innovations. One new feature was mechanical ventilation. This was effected by steam-driven fans which produced a slight positive air pressure on the gundeck. Clearing powder smoke to enable gunners to see the target was as much a concern as habitability of the lower decks.

La Gloire and *Warrior* were not alone. The French built four more ships like *La Gloire*, and *Warrior* was quickly followed by a sister ship and a succession of eight more even larger ironclads.

When first completed, the British ironclads were invulnerable. No other nation had the means to stop them.

---

[1] Iron rusts very much less readily than steel. *Great Britain*'s hull is composed of wrought iron plates a half-inch thick, lapped and rivetted. Roughly fifty percent of their thickness survives.

[2] Kinburn is not, as it sounds, a castle in Scotland but a fortress covering the mouth of the River Dnieper.

WAR AS A SPUR TO DESIGN DEVELOPMENT

In wartime conditions new technology is applied and new designs are introduced to meet what are suddenly perceived as urgent needs. The Crimean War brought forth rapid development in small steam warships called gunboats, which had a profound influence on ideas of naval construction, and in due course on worldwide politics in the second half of the century.

In the American Civil War that followed, the speculative ideas of John Ericsson were at last given the chance of realization. The whole concept of the low-freeboard shallow-draft armored ship was exploited with speed and resourcefulness. The Civil War saw the use of a variety of novel warship types improvised to meet the occasion, and out of the war came another new type of warship, the screw-propelled cruiser, which also took on a life of its own.

Gunboats

Gunboats were designed for close blockade, for coastal bombardment and supporting landings, for carrying dispatches, and for survey work. During the Crimean War the British used them most effectively in the Sea of Azov, which largely separates the Crimean peninsula from the Russian mainland. Gunboats raided twenty towns along its shores in order to destroy the supply lines, and indeed the very economic base of the Russian army in the peninsula.

In the Baltic gunboats and mortar-vessels took part with the fleet in the assault on the island of Bomarsund in the Aland Islands in 1854, and next year led the bombardment of Sveaborg, the Russian naval base just off Helsinki. Sveaborg was largely destroyed by mortar fire, but the multi-tiered stone batteries on the island of Kronstadt guarding the approaches to St. Petersburg were judged too powerful to attack in 1855. A far more formidable force of vessels designed for coastal assault was assembled by the Royal Navy ready for the campaign season of 1856. It was the threat to the seat of government represented by this fleet that was a major factor in obliging Russia to sue for peace after the loss of Sevastopol.

The Crimean War gunboat was a 100-foot-long screw steamer of 230 tons displacement with a wooden hull, three masts, and schooner rig. It had a speed of eight knots and mounted two heavy guns. The guns, 68-pounder muzzle-loading rifles, were on the centerline, mounted on pivots; they could be swung to fire on either beam. The gun carriage fitted to a slot which enabled it to be trained through an arc of sixty degrees, pointing through a gunport in the bulwarks. The big line-of-battle ships were provided with "bow chasers" and "stern chasers" fore and aft on the weather deck, mounted in the same way.

The so-called armored batteries were an enlargement of the gunboat design. Screw-ships, 180 feet long and twice the displacement of the gunboats, they carried an armament of sixteen 68-pounders behind ports along the broadsides.

Four and a half years after the fall of Sevastopol fighting broke out in the American Civil War. All kinds of

Plate 12.

USS *Pontoosuc*
Fort Fisher, North Carolina, 1865

A total of forty-seven "double-enders" was built for the U.S. Navy during the Civil War. They were side-wheel paddle steamers with a rudder at each end, designed to operate in narrow waters where they could find themselves in a vulnerable situation if they were obliged to try to turn around.

The *Pontoosuc* is representative of the type. She was one of twenty-eight vessels in the *Sassacus* class, wooden built and massively armed. Their displacement was 1,173 tons, they were 240 feet long and thirty-five feet in the beam, and their inclined direct-acting engines could drive them at thirteen knots.

Pontoosuc was built by the George W. Lawrence Company of Thomaston, Maine, and engined by the Portland Locomotive Works. She was laid down in 1862, launched the next year, and completed in May 1864. Her armament started off as two 100-pounder muzzle-loading rifles, four nine-inch smoothbores, two 20-pounder rifles, two 24-pounder howitzers, and one 12-pounder. Later one of the 100-pounder rifles was replaced by an eleven-inch smoothbore cannon.

The gunboat was first employed in the Gulf of St. Lawrence, searching for the raider CSS *Tallahassee*, and in December 1864 she was one of seven double-enders engaged in the unsuccessful assault on Fort Fisher, North Carolina. In February 1865 she took part in the reduction of the fort.

Note the canvas wind-scoops which were rigged on the masts to try to funnel fresh air down to the men toiling in the stokehold and engine room below decks. The bulwarks have been lowered in places to allow a field of fire to the gunboat's grim cast-iron artillery pieces.

Plate 13.

USS *Monitor*, CSS *Virginia*, and USS *Minnesota*

Hampton Roads, Virginia, 1862

On Sunday morning, March 9, 1862, the Confederate ironclad CSS *Virginia* (ex-USS *Merrimack*), sallied out for the second day from the mouth of the Elizabeth River. She headed for the screw sloop USS *Minnesota* which was lying helplessly stranded near the shore on the north side of Hampton Roads. *Minnesota* had run aground the day before.

On Saturday the *Virginia* had thrown the U.S. Navy into some confusion, having rammed and sunk the frigate USS *Cumberland* and destroyed the USS *Congress* by gunfire. Confidently expecting to renew her successful attacks on one wooden ship after another, the ironclad found herself intercepted by a most extraordinary rival.

The newcomer was a tiny ironclad which had joined the U.S. squadron in Chesapeake Bay overnight. Her name was USS *Monitor* and she had reached the scene of action under tow from New York.

The painting shows the contrast in size between *Monitor* (172 feet long) and *Virginia* (263 feet in length). What cannot be seen is that below water level *Virginia* has a deep-draft wooden hull: the screw frigate *Merrimack*, on whose wooden bottom *Virginia*'s armored casemate was constructed, had originally looked much like *Minnesota* on the right of the painting.

Monitor was a warship of totally new conception, with a shallow-draft hull of composite wood and iron construction which enabled her to move freely through the shallows. Her armored turret proved impermeable to *Virginia*'s mixed battery of rifles and smoothbores.

Unfortunately the *Monitor* had been given instructions to use no more than half-charges in her two eleven-inch smoothbore cannon. Consequently her gunfire was especially ineffectual against *Virginia*'s armored casemate, even at point-blank range. Nevertheless her intervention effectively stopped the Confederate ironclad's adventure.

Historically, the duel was notable as the first combat between armored ships.

Plate 14.

USS *New Ironsides*
on the Delaware River, 1862

Named for "Old Ironsides," the wooden frigate USS *Constitution* which covered herself with glory in the War of 1812, USS *New Ironsides* was the most powerful unit in the U.S. Navy during the Civil War. She is portrayed as she swept grandly down the Delaware past New Castle to join the fleet in August 1862. She has just emerged from the renowned shipyard of C.H. and W.H. Cramp in Philadelphia.

Her masts and rigging were later shorn to the deck and the smokestack cut down before she was taken into action against Confederate shore defenses before Charleston in 1863. She was again engaged in action at Fort Fisher, North Carolina, in December 1864 and early 1865.

USS *Maratanza*, a side-wheel paddle gunboat built in Boston in 1861, is thrashing upriver on the port side of the ironclad.

New Ironsides saw extensive service in the war and was hit by dozens of projectiles fired by Confederate shore artillery. She also had a spar torpedo prodded into her by CSS *David* off Charleston in October 1863. In all this, she suffered no serious damage.

The ironclad was timber built, with four-inch wrought iron cladding on the sides for most of her length, only the extreme bow and stern portions remaining unprotected. Her armament comprised two 150-pounder rifles, two 50-pounders, and fourteen eleven-inch smoothbore cannon. Her shortcoming was lack of power: her engines were capable of no more than six knots.

Unfortunately she was accidentally destroyed by fire at League Island in 1866.

Maratanza saw widespread war service, capturing a Confederate balloon tender in the James River and taking five blockade-runners as prizes. After the war she was sold as a merchantman, sold again, and served for a time in the Haitian Navy.

ships were pressed into service, and new types were hastily devised to meet the needs of this kind of war. Gunboats were required for river service in support of the armies. Many were converted from existing river steamers and others were built from scratch.

The majority of Union ships constructed for river service were the "double-enders." Paddlers, they were equipped with rudders at bow as well as stern to enable them to retire without attempting to turn in the width of a river. The double-enders were wooden-built vessels more than 200 feet long with heavy armament, usually including six large-caliber guns mounted on swivels on the top deck.

The campaign in the West prompted the construction of shallow-draft warships on the Mississippi, many of them armored craft. Seven river ironclads built by James Eads at St. Louis were protected by two-and-one-half-inch-thick iron casemates, and a dozen armored gunboats of other designs were built upriver for use by Union forces. There were also a large number of conversions, some of which were armored but more of which were clad with light sheet iron or with timber as protection against small-arms fire. These vessels were known as "tinclads" and "timberclads."

Gunboats continued to be built throughout the nineteenth century. They became larger and more seaworthy; some acquired barquentine rig—a combination of fore-and-aft and square sails—and some had hoisting screws and other aids to long-range cruising. They were the most

economical warships to send on missions where there were local political or commercial objectives to be supported, and they were the only type of vessel which could move deep into the interior up the great rivers of the world. Gunboats were even transported overland and assembled on the Great Lakes of Africa and above the cataracts on the Congo and the Nile. Some 370 were built for the Royal Navy alone.

Monitors

Both sides in the American Civil War recognized the significance of the recent development in Europe of armored ships. A navy equipped with ironclads would be able to seize command of the sea.

The Union entered the war with the whole U.S. Navy at its disposal, but many of the principal units were stranded in the Navy Yard at Norfolk, Virginia, and had to be sabotaged before the yard was abandoned to Southern forces. The line-of-battle ships took no part in the fighting, but twenty surviving frigates, half of them steamers, plus half a dozen sloops were available to carry the war to the coasts of the Confederacy.

The federal government immediately ordered the construction of three ironclads. These three ships were diverse in design and their fortunes were varied. The one that achieved fame was called USS *Monitor*.

John Ericsson, the pioneer of screw propulsion who had been rebuffed in his attempt to get his ideas adopted in England, had long been germinating a radical design for warships. In the emergency of the times, and with the help of enthusiastic friends, he managed to win approval from the Navy to build a prototype. Construction was rushed forward in Brooklyn, New York, and the ship was ready within four months.

Ericsson named the *Monitor* from the dictionary definition "to check and control." He called her a fighting machine. She was only 170 feet long and her raft-like hull of composite wood and iron construction floated largely

Plate 15.

USS *Lehigh* and USS *Sangamon*
on the James River, Virginia, 1863

The U.S. Navy carried out a tremendous building program during the Civil War, starting construction of more than 200 vessels and acquiring 418. The majority of the larger new ships were wooden screw sloops and gunboats, and a great number of paddle steamers were built or converted for river operations.

The most remarkable development in naval construction was the evolution of the monitor as a type, modeled on Ericsson's pioneering craft. Twenty-two monitors were completed and put into commission before the war's end (many more were under construction). They were armored ships with very low freeboard, and they used screw propulsion with the screw well protected from enemy fire under the raft-like hull. The only features above the armored deck were a cylindrical armored revolving turret, usually mounting two large-caliber muzzle-loading smoothbore guns, and a prominent smokestack. Five of the vessels had two turrets.

Two of the ten-strong *Passaic* class monitors are seen in the James River.

Their principal scenes of operations were before Charleston, in the James River, and at the mouth of the Cape Fear River, Wilmington, North Carolina.

The principal armament was slow to train and had an agonizingly slow rate of fire. To protect themselves against boarders, therefore, the monitors carried light field guns on deck which could be rapidly wheeled into action and brought to bear on approaching small craft.

submerged. Not more than a foot showed above the water.

This was a ship designed with a specific, limited purpose: to meet and destroy another ironclad. On the raft was mounted a cylindrical revolving turret. The turret carried just two guns, Dahlgren eleven-inch caliber smooth-bore muzzle-loaders, and the turret armor was eight inches thick. The turret ship presented a minimal target, and if she could get close enough her massive cannon should have been able to blast through any contemporary armor. *Monitor*'s displacement was less than 1,000 tons, her speed was nine knots, her endurance was limited, and her field of action was restricted to sheltered waters.

Ericsson's craft barely managed the passage from New York to Chesapeake Bay under tow, and nine months after her encounter at Hampton Roads she foundered in a gale while on the way to Charleston, South Carolina.

But the ironclad accomplished her intended role. In March 1862 she intercepted the Confederate ironclad *Virginia* off Norfolk. The fighting machine proved invulnerable to shells fired by seven-inch rifles or nine-inch smoothbores at point-blank range. Her own guns, mistakenly, had been restricted to the use of half-charges and were unable to make an impression on the enemy. The encounter became a standoff, but it was a strategic rebuff for the Confederacy. *Monitor* prevented the breaking of the Union blockade, continuation of which was a major factor in the eventual defeat of the South.

The other two Union ironclads ordered at the outbreak of war were very different. USS *New Ironsides* was an oceangoing ship, a broadside ironclad of 4,100 tons. She carried a heavy armament of two 150-pounder and two 50-pounder rifles and fourteen eleven-inch smoothbores. The hull was built of oak twelve inches thick at the waterline, covered by an extensive four-inch armored belt, but her engines were good for only six knots. The ship was the most powerful unit in the U.S. Navy and is notable for having been the first-ever target of torpedo attack. She was only slightly damaged by a spar torpedo which was rammed into her by the tiny torpedo boat CSS *David* in October 1863. *New Ironsides* continued to play an active role in the war;

her armor was shown to be effective in resisting damage from dozens of enemy hits. She survived the war, but was accidentally destroyed by fire in December 1866.

The third ironclad was called USS *Galena*. She was a ship the size of *Monitor* with a broadside armament and a rudimentary form of iron protection. Her armor proved ineffectual in action.

Monitor's immunity from cannon fire made a great impression on the Navy, and a large number of new ships was ordered along the same lines. Before the end of the war some twenty *Monitor* type ships had joined the fleet, and this class of vessel comprised the main force of the Navy for the next thirty years.

A Confederate Battle Fleet

The Confederacy entered the war without a navy, and immediately all sorts of merchant vessels were pressed into naval use. Many more were employed as blockade runners or privateers. The South was far more dependent on imports than the North, and just as vital was the need to maintain its cotton export trade. The government quickly seized on the possibility of reversing its naval inferiority by creating a fleet of ironclads. There were only scarce domestic resources to do the job, so $2 million were appropriated for buying or building ships abroad.

The Confederate ironclads which saw action, however, were reach-me-downs. The first was CSS *Virginia*. This vessel was contrived out of the hull of the screw frigate USS *Merrimack*, which had been burned when Norfolk was abandoned. The timber hull was cut down to form a platform for an armored casemate battery protected by two layers of two-inch bars forged from railroad tracks. The hull was almost completely submerged. *Virginia*'s displacement was 3,200 tons, more than three times that of *Monitor*.

The makeshift warship, like the *Monitor*, had limited speed and endurance, but with her mixed armament of rifles and smoothbores and her iron ram she proved more than a match in sheltered waters for the Union screw frigates

Plate 16.

USS *Kearsarge*
Boulogne, France, 1864

After her long and destructive cruise in the Atlantic and Indian oceans, the Confederate raider CSS *Alabama* put into the port of Cherbourg in France for repairs. The U.S. Navy sent the screw sloop USS *Kearsarge* to lie off the port and attack the *Alabama* when she regained the open sea.

The Confederate captain sent an impertinent message to the Yankee begging him not to depart before he could get his ship out of harbor. On 19 June 1864 the *Alabama* emerged and made straight for the *Kearsarge*, followed by a flotilla of French spectators.

The engagement was not prolonged. The *Kearsarge*'s more modern armament, including two eleven-inch Dahlgren smoothbores, soon hammered the *Alabama* into sinking condition, and the crew of the raider surrendered before their ship sank by the stern. *Alabama*'s gunfire was partly ineffectual due to deterioration of her powder supply during her long period at sea.

Since the *Kearsarge*'s boats were all smashed in action, *Alabama*'s survivors were rescued by one of the spectator ships. The victorious U.S. warship steamed into Boulogne to effect repairs.

The *Kearsarge* was a wooden sloop built at Portsmouth Navy Yard, Kittery, Maine. She was one of the *Mohican* class, built under the emergency war program, and she mounted in addition to the big smoothbores four 32-pounder cannon and a 30-pounder rifle.

She had an active career, subsequently serving on the South Pacific, the Asiatic, the North Atlantic, and the West Indies stations. She was wrecked on Roncador Reef, Central America, in 1894.

which were pitted against her.

Virginia's success provoked further orders, and in the course of the war a dozen shallow-draft ironclads were converted or built in the South for river use. The overseas purchasing mission failed in its effort to buy La Gloire, but five armored ships were laid down to order in private French and British yards. Diplomatic efforts by the Union succeeded in preventing the delivery of all but one of these ships.

Only one foreign-built ironclad, CSS Stonewall, was eventually commissioned into the Confederate Navy. She was one of six warships built for the South by the ship-builder Arman of Bordeaux, two of them ironclads and the rest intended as commerce-raiding cruisers. As a result of Federal intervention all the ships were sold by the builders to other countries. The ironclad Sphinx was sold to Denmark, but with the end of their war with Prussia the Danes canceled the contract and she was secretly repurchased by the Confederate agent. Given her new name Stonewall, she sailed under Confederate colors from Ferrol in northwest Spain in January 1865. Two U.S. warships had been sent with orders to intercept her, the wooden screw frigate Niagara and the sloop Sacramento.

Stonewall had a displacement of only 1,400 tons and was seriously outgunned by her opponents, but she had the protection of a four-and-one-half-inch-thick armored belt. Captain Thomas Craven of the Niagara declined to tackle the ironclad, and she was allowed to cross the Atlantic. By the time Stonewall reached Cuba, however, the war was over. Her captain impudently sold her to the Spanish Captain-General, who promptly handed her over to the United States. The ironclad was later sold to the Shōgun of Japan, but on arrival at Yokohama in 1868 she was seized by the Emperor. Renamed Koketsu, she took part in the attack on the Shōgun's stronghold and then continued serving in the Imperial Japanese Navy until the end of the century.

The most formidable of the intended Confederate ironclads were two rams built by Lairds of Birkenhead. They were seagoing ships twice the size of Stonewall, with twin nine-inch rifled guns in each of two revolving turrets. The turrets were mounted on the main deck, protected from heavy seas by bulwarks which could be lowered to provide a clear field of fire in action. Both ships were seized and found their way into the Royal Navy. HMS Scorpion (ex-North Carolina) served for years as a guard ship at Bermuda and HMS Wivern (ex-Mississippi) filled the same role at Hong Kong.

The possession of a squadron of fast and seaworthy ironclads would have transformed the naval prospects of the South, and could have had a decisive effect on the course of the war. This would never have been achieved by commerce raiders alone: ultimately only a contest of battle fleets could secure command of the sea.

The Origins of the Cruiser

The Civil War precipitated another development in warship design, the evolution of the commerce-raiding cruiser. The South pressed all sorts of vessels into service in an attempt to divert Union warships from the blockade. Sixteen steamers were bought or built abroad for Confederate service, three of which pursued successful careers on the high seas in search of Union merchant vessels. CSS Alabama, in particular, ranged the South Atlantic and the Indian Ocean as well as European waters and took sixty prizes in a period of eighteen months.

The notorious raider was a wooden-built screw steamer with a speed of thirteen knots. Her armament was one seven-inch rifle, an eight-inch (68-pounder), and six 32-pounder smoothbores. She was sunk in short order when she was eventually caught by USS Kearsarge, largely due to the fact that by this time her powder had deteriorated.

The disruption to trade and the indignity caused by these exploits focused the attention of the U.S. Navy on opportunities for commerce raiding as a means of warfare. Before the end of the Civil War half a dozen cruisers were laid down. They were wooden-built screw steamers, long, lean vessels with a displacement of 3,900-4,200 tons, packed with machinery. They were strongly armed with ten nine-inch smoothbores on the broadsides and two or three rifled 60-pounders on the upper deck. In the event of British intervention they were to harry her mercantile trade, and they were designed to outstrip the troublesome Confederate raiders.

Best known of the Union cruisers was USS *Wampanoag*. She created a sensation when she averaged seventeen knots on trials, the fastest recorded to that time. She was a striking ship with four funnels grouped in pairs and three masts supporting light fore-and-aft rig. The cruiser had a straight stem, unlike the graceful clipper bow which was almost universal on warships of the day. Like many ships built during the war she suffered from the use of unseasoned timber. *Wampanoag* had a service career of less than nine months, but she and her sister ships had a far-reaching effect on naval architecture.

Mines, Torpedoes, Submarines, and Rams

The Crimean War saw the first operational use of underwater mines. Three British warships operating in the Baltic, near the Russian naval base at Kronstadt, were damaged by mines moored below the surface. The mines were of two types, contact mines and remotely controlled ones. The explosive charges were small and they caused little damage, but from this time onwards the threat of mines began to exert a greater and greater influence on naval strategy. Experiments with submersibles were carried out by both British and Russian navies but they never reached operational status.

In the Civil War the Confederacy used mines with mixed success. (Confusingly, the term torpedo was used for what we would now call a mine.) One instance was during the Battle of Mobile Bay in 1864. The assault on the harbor mouth had been delayed for nine months pending the arrival with the U.S. fleet of ironclads which would be a match for the Confederate vessels.

Admiral David Farragut led the attack in the wooden screw sloop USS *Hartford*. Warned of the presence of mines

he scornfully ordered "Damn the torpedoes, full speed ahead." The monitor USS *Tecumseh*, steaming straight for the enemy, struck a mine and sank with heavy loss of life, but the rest of the U.S. fleet forced the passage past the forts and destroyed or captured all the Confederate ships.

Two other U.S. monitors were sunk by mines, but an attempt to sink the big ironclad USS *New Ironsides* at Charleston by means of a remotely controlled mine was unsuccessful.

Spar torpedoes were employed by both sides. They consisted of an explosive charge mounted on a long pole which was pushed into the side of an enemy ship. The Confederate ironclad CSS *Albemarle* was sunk at night in the Roanoke River by a small craft armed with a spar torpedo.

The Confederate Navy built sixteen torpedo boats and they made half a dozen torpedo attacks on Federal ships. Called "davids," they were 50-foot-long wooden vessels, designed to operate partly submerged. Three fully submersible boats were also employed by the Confederacy, and a submersible was built and tested during the war by the U.S. Navy.

One of the three Confederate submersibles, CSS *H.L. Hunley*, made history by sinking the screw sloop USS *Housatonic* off Charleston in 1864, but she herself was destroyed simultaneously by the explosion of her own spar torpedo.

These craft were only at the very threshold of operational effectiveness. Many crew members died in unsuccessful diving trials of *H.L. Hunley* and another boat was swamped in action. The third boat, *Pioneer I*, survived and can be seen at the Louisiana State Museum.

Of all the naval developments hastened by the Crimean and the Civil wars, it was the birth of underwater warfare which had the most far-reaching consequences.

This was not the case with the ram. Steam power coupled with armor protection seemed to designers to offer the prospect of using ships themselves as assault weapons. The case seemed strengthened by the ramming and sinking of the screw frigate USS *Cumberland* by CSS *Virginia*.

HMS *Camperdown* 1888

Thereafter few ironclads were built without some consideration for ramming in the design of the bow. Success was achieved in 1866 at the Battle of Lissa, when the Austrian flagship *Erzherzhog* rammed and sank the Italian ironclad *Re d'Italia*. The Italian ship was a sister of USS *New Ironsides*, one of two that had been built in New York and supplied to the Italian Navy.

The result at Lissa was a delusion, for the Italian fleet was in disarray and the victim had already been disabled when she was struck. Careful analysis showed that successful ramming tactics required an unlikely margin of superior speed or an enemy who had lost the power of maneuver. The increasing range and power of naval gunnery further reduced the likelihood of success.

The principal outcome of the vogue for ram bows was a number of disastrous peacetime collisions. In 1875 the ironclad HMS *Iron Duke* accidentally rammed her sister ship *Vanguard* in a fog off Dublin Bay, tearing a hole below the armor and causing her to sink within an hour. In 1878

the Prussian fleet flagship SMS *König Wilhelm* rammed her consort *Grosser Kurfürst* in the English Channel while maneuvering to avoid a sailing ship. The injured vessel sank with heavy loss of life.

In 1893 occurred the notorious collision between HMS *Victoria* and *Camperdown* off what is now Lebanon. The flagship of the Mediterranean Fleet was rammed and sunk by the flagship of the second division while the fleet was conducting a deliberate evolution in clear weather. At first sight the circumstances suggest supreme negligence on the part of the Commander in Chief, who was lost with his ship. The court-martial proceedings, however, suggest that the witnesses closed ranks—being reluctant to throw blame on the surviving admiral—and from what we know of the personalities of the two men it seems likely that the careful phrasing of the C-in-C's signal went beyond the comprehension of his second-in-command. *Victoria* sank almost immediately with half of her crew of 700, and *Camperdown* was badly damaged.

Plate 17.

CSS *Stonewall*, USS *Sacramento*, and USS *Niagara*

off Ferrol, Spain, 1865

Out of five ironclads ordered from French and British yards by the Confederacy only one was eventually commissioned and sailed under Confederate colors. She was the *Stonewall*, built by Arman of Bordeaux. When she set out to cross the Atlantic she was intercepted by two U.S. warships, the wooden screw frigate *Niagara*, under the command of Captain Craven, and the sloop *Sacramento*.

The Confederate ship had a displacement of only 1,400 tons and was seriously outgunned by her antagonists, but she had the protection of a four-and-a-half-inch-thick armored belt. Captain Craven declined to tackle the ironclad and she was allowed to cross the Atlantic, where she headed for Cuba. By the time she reached Havana the war was over, and the Spanish Captain-General took possession of the ship and handed her over to the United States government.

Stonewall lay for some time at Washington Navy Yard and was later sold to the Shōgun of Japan. On arrival at Yokohama in 1868 she was seized by the Emperor. Renamed *Koketsu*, she took part in the attack on the Shōgun's stronghold, and then continued to serve as a unit in the Imperial Japanese Navy until the end of the nineteenth century.

Plate 18.

König Wilhelm
Kiel, Germany, 1870

A fine example of the broadside ironclad, the 11,000-ton screw steamer *König Wilhelm* was built by the Thames Iron Works at Millwall in London. She was designed by Sir Edward Reed and was originally intended for the Turkish Navy. Bought on the stocks by the Prussian government, she was for many years the largest and most powerful ship in the Prussian Navy.

In 1878 she was part of a squadron steaming up the Channel which encountered a merchant ship at close quarters. As a result of an error in helm orders *König Wilhelm* rammed the turret ship *Grosser Kürfurst* and sank her with heavy loss of life.

König Wilhelm had an armament of eighteen 9.4-inch guns in broadside casemates, plus five 8.3-inch guns. Her wrought iron belt was up to twelve inches thick and her deck armor was two inches. She had a horizontal single expansion engine, a single screw, and could make 14.7 knots.

In common with many ships of her kind she underwent reconstruction in the 1890s, being re-boilered and losing her tall square-sail rig. She was recommissioned as an armored cruiser, with an improved secondary armament and enlarged coal supply.

The ironclad became a school ship to the Naval Academy after 1907 and was not sold out of the Navy until 1921.

BROADSIDE BATTERY IRONCLADS, TURRET SHIPS, AND PRE-DREADNOUGHTS

The first use of revolving armored turrets in action took place in the American Civil War. From today's vantage point the benefits of the turret seem overwhelming. The same guns can be brought to bear on either beam, fire can be directed over a wide arc, and guns and gun crew are protected from enemy fire. John Ericsson was not alone in his conviction: Captain Cowper Coles in Britain had taken out patents for the design of turrets and his first was tried out on board ship in 1861. Coles' turret traversed on a path of roller bearings which was secure from enemy fire, whereas Ericsson's rotated a little uncertainly on an elevating central pivot.

At the time, however, the advantages of turrets of any kind were not so self-evident. Muzzle-loading cannon of the day were inaccurate, and they possessed an agonizingly slow rate of fire. It took about eight minutes between discharges to reload *Monitor*'s pair of guns. A well-served line-of-battle ship could deliver a storm of fire in the same period.

The weight of armored turrets was such that they could be mounted no more than a few feet above the waterline without endangering the stability of the ship. A low freeboard ship was severely constrained by the condition of the sea, and guns which were carried close to the water level quickly became unworkable in heavy weather.

Consequently the broadside battery layout was not immediately superseded. Evolution in ship design proceeded in parallel with developments in guns and gunnery. Bigger guns were countered by thicker armor and by improvements

in the layout and quality of protection.

The high freeboard ship with its guns firing through ports in the hull was modified with a view to providing wider fields of fire, particularly forward and aft. The battery was concentrated amidships, enabling heavier armor to be applied over this limited length and leaving the ends of the ship without protection.

The manufacture of heavier guns with greater range meant that a ship could afford to carry fewer of them. They were brought together in an armored citadel, with gunports bearing obliquely to allow fore and aft fire as well as on the broadside. In some ships the hull was cut away to form embrasures, in some the battery was projected over the side of the ship, and in others the hull was given an exaggerated tumble home.[1] If the upper deck was made considerably narrower than the hull at the waterline, gun positions could be built out from the upper deck and enjoy a clear field of fire through 180 degrees. Bow chasers and stern chasers were generally mounted on the upper deck.

The usual scheme of protection was a vertical belt at the waterline of six-inch to twelve-inch-thick iron on heavy wooden backing, plus armor on the sides of the citadel and armored bulkheads enclosing it.

Central battery ironclads, as they became termed, carried full sailing rig and they often had telescopic funnels and lifting screws. They were seaworthy, they had great endurance, and they were capable of up to about fifteen knots under power. One of the last of the central battery ships, the French *Rédoutable*, was laid down in 1873. She

Plate 19.

HMS *Northumberland*
Malta, 1869

The high, broad stern of an eighteenth century line-of-battle ship used to be elaborately decorated. A row of great windows lighted the cabins of the captain and the flag officer, if one was aboard. This attractive feature made the ship vulnerable to fire from an enemy vessel passing close across the stern. Cannon shot could be directed through the stern windows and rake the gundecks from end to end.

Nineteenth century ironclads were protected by rounded, armored sterns. In order to compensate the captain for the loss of his handsome stern windows it became the custom to provide a wrought-iron balcony around the stern, with access through French windows on either side of the principal cabin. This "sternwalk," as it became termed, provided a sheltered promenade which gave the captain the opportunity of absolute privacy, a rarity on board ship.

Sternwalks continued to be fitted to larger British warships until about 1915, and one or two were still to be seen at the time of the Second World War.

No such frippery would be allowed on a modern warship, but in some ships the captain's cabin alone enjoys the light of day through a scuttle (that is to say, a porthole). This is the last vestige of the privilege provided by a sternwalk.

was the first ship to be built of steel framing, but her armor cladding was still composed of wrought iron on teak.

The turret ship followed its own path of evolution. The Royal Navy converted one of the wooden liners to a turret ship in 1862. Her name was HMS *Royal Sovereign*; she was cut down from a 120-gun three-decker and given an armored belt and four turrets with ten-inch guns. Her role, like that of the monitors, was not only coastal defense but also assault. The later Civil War monitors had two turrets instead of one, and, more importantly, the later ships had twin shafts and screws with separate engines. This development bestowed a critical improvement in reliability.

In order to provide better seaworthiness than monitors, the turret ships built by Lairds in England were equipped with forecastles and sterns above the level of the turret deck, and hinged bulwarks could be folded flat to allow a field of fire in action. Tubular tripod masts were adopted in order to reduce the interference caused by standing rigging.

Coles, the protagonist of turrets, was critical of the turret ships then being built for the Royal Navy. Typical of these was the *Monarch*, designed by Sir Edward Reed and completed in 1869. Coles used his position as a Member of Parliament to agitate for the building of ships to Lairds' design, and against Reed's bitter opposition the Admiralty finally agreed.

The outcome was a ship called the *Captain*. *Monarch*'s turrets were carried some fourteen feet above sea level, but *Captain*'s deck was less than seven feet above the water. Unlike the American monitors, which had a freeboard measured in inches rather than feet, she was ship-rigged, designed for ocean passage. *Captain* had a raised superstructure over most of the length of the hull, connected by a so-called "flying" deck which bridged across the turrets.

The combination of low freeboard and full rig proved disastrous. In November 1870 she was caught in a sudden squall in the Bay of Biscay, heeled beyond safety, and capsized. Most of the crew was lost with the ship, including Captain Coles.

Plate 20.

HMS *Devastation*
Malta, 1875

Seminal ship design of the ironclad era, *Devastation* bore the seeds of growth of the battleship idea. She had twin screws and two sets of engines, which finally made it possible to dispense with the whole paraphernalia of sailing rig; she was an oceangoing ship with substantial endurance under steam; she had an armored deck which was tied-in to the top edge of the thick belt of waterline armor on her sides; and her big guns were mounted in two revolving turrets fore and aft with wide arcs of fire. None of these features alone was entirely new, but the combination was incomparable. *Devastation* outmatched the all-round capability of any other fighting ship, and she became the model for the design of capital ships until well into the twentieth century.

Devastation was completed in 1873, and the ironclad makes an interesting comparison with a traditional wooden ship-of-the-line, part of which can be glimpsed through the ancient fortifications of the Knights of St. John at Malta.

With the increasing efficiency and reliability of steam power, and above all with the adoption of twin engines and screws, it became no longer necessary to provide sailing rig to bring a ship to port in the event of breakdown. Reed, before he resigned from office in protest over the decision to build *Captain*, had designed a true oceangoing turreted ironclad. She was given the name *Devastation*, and she could fairly be described as the world's first battleship.

Devastation was completed in 1873. She was a twin-screw vessel with a speed of fourteen knots and a range of 4,700 miles, and she dispensed entirely with sailing rig. A single central mast was provided to support a fighting top, signal yards, and a derrick for handling the ship's boats. Her displacement was 9,300 tons, much the same as *Warrior*'s.

Devastation's iron protection accounted for no less than twenty-four percent of her displacement. Her turret armor was fourteen inches thick laid over eighteen-inch teak, and most significantly she had three-inch horizontal armor at the main deck level (the top of the belt), plus a two-inch shelter deck.

Devastation marks a watershed in the development of ironclads. She embodied all the new technology of the century, and after her there remained room only for refinement and improvement.

Trunk engines were superseded in later ships by vertical reciprocating engines and later by compound types for better economy, and fire-tube boilers gave way to water-tube boilers capable of higher pressures. Muzzle-loading rifled guns were replaced by breechloaders, then by long-barrelled guns using improved propellant. Steel took the place of iron, and techniques of face-hardening steel, coupled with new alloys, provided greater resistance in armor of no greater thickness than before. The pre-Dreadnought battleships of the 1890s were far more powerful warships than *Devastation*, but they followed the lines first laid down in her design.

The Italian Navy, shocked by its mauling at the hands of the Austrians at the Battle of Lissa, determined to build new ships which would be able to overcome any vessel they might meet. The country lacked the resources to match the navy of a major maritime power, but individual ships would be superior, and they were to have the speed to decline action if outnumbered.

Two large ironclads were laid down in 1873. It was intended to arm them with the biggest available guns, 12.5-inch caliber (38-ton) muzzle-loaders from the British firm of Armstrong. The armaments company, eager for business, offered something better. The ships were seven years in construction, and before completion they were provided by Armstrong with monstrous cannon, 17.7-inch caliber (100-ton) weapons which could penetrate any existing armor. The guns took a quarter of an hour to reload between shots.

The Italian ships, *Duilio* and *Dandolo*, were provided with commensurate protection. Their armor belt was for the first time composed of steel, which had hitherto been used only for ships' framing. The French company Le Creusot had developed the technique; they supplied twenty-two-inch-thick armor plating for the hull and seventeen-inch nickel-steel alloy for the two twin turrets. Resistance was almost twice as great as for the same thickness of iron.

Duilio and *Dandolo*, designed by Benedetto Brin, were 11,000-ton ships with a speed of more than fifteen knots. *Duilio* housed in her stern a torpedo boat which could be released to attack with two fourteen-inch Whitehead torpedoes.

News of the Italian plans drew attention in Whitehall. There was a direct response. A ship called HMS *Inflexible* was built to match the Italians, broad in the beam, prodigiously well armored, and mounting guns almost as large as theirs. She was the last to be given full sailing rig and almost the last with muzzle-loaders, but she was also full of innovations such as electric lights and anti-roll tanks.

Inflexible's armor was a compound of layers of iron and steel with a heavy wood backing, an incredible forty-one inches in thickness at its maximum along the sides at the waterline. For the first time protection was organized on the principle of "all or nothing": in place of graduated thicknesses of armor throughout the length of the hull only the vital machinery and magazine spaces were given side

IHM

HMS Inflexible 1881

armor, but this was of maximum thickness. The ends of the ship were protected only by a three-inch armored deck below water level.

The development of slow-burning propellant made possible great strides in gunnery. Gun barrels became longer to allow for the buildup of higher muzzle velocity, and this conferred increased range, accuracy, and penetrating power. The French developed the interrupted-screw design which at last provided a reliable opening-breech mechanism. Several navies adopted breech-loading before the Royal Navy finally reverted to breechloaders in 1879.

Inflexible was really an experimental design; she was too extreme to become a satisfactory model for evolution. It was decided that big guns would be better mounted in the open, on top of circular armored redoubts which came to be called barbettes. (The French term for guns mounted in this fashion was *en barbette*.) Eliminating the weight of turrets made it possible to move the guns a whole deck higher,

where they were well clear of interference from heavy seas and enjoyed superior command of a remote target.

The new threat of attack by torpedo boats led to the need for a secondary battery of "quick-firing" guns—six-inch, 6-pounders, and 3-pounders. These smaller guns had been developed using small-arms practice, with an integral cartridge case and projectile. (The great size and weight of ammunition for heavy guns made it necessary to load charge and projectile separately, and this is still the case with USS *Iowa*'s sixteen-inch guns in 1993.)

The new design philosophy was embodied in British ships of the *Admiral* class, completed in 1887 to 1889. Their big guns were mounted in pairs fore and aft, as in *Devastation*, and the quick-firers were concentrated in a compact central superstructure. The French *Térrible* and the Italian *Italia* classes also adopted the use of open barbettes for the principal armament.

The mainstream of development is represented by

Plate 21.

Dandolo
La Spezia, Italy, 1882

Armed with two pairs of giant 17.7-inch guns, *Dandolo* and her sister ship *Duilio* caused a considerable stir when they joined the Italian Navy. The only ships ever to carry larger caliber guns were the Japanese *Musashi* and *Yamato* of 1942 and the British *Furious* of 1917.

Nothing at sea in 1882 could resist the sledgehammer blows from the Italians' Armstrong muzzle-loading rifled guns, but their rate of fire was only one round in fifteen minutes.

Dandolo was also very heavily armored. She was the first in the world with steel, 12.5-inch maximum thickness armor; the plates were supplied by the French firm Le Creusot, together with nickel steel armor to the central citadel and turrets. She was subdivided into eighty-three watertight compartments and had cellular rafts at bow and stern below the armored deck.

The two twin turrets were disposed *en échelon*, to starboard and port amidships, to enable a degree of end-on fire as well as to allow all four guns to be trained on either beam. The armament included three thirteen-inch torpedo tubes and light guns. Later in her career the main battery was reduced to four ten-inch and supplemented by a large secondary and tertiary armament. She was used as a stationary harbor defense in the First World War.

On the right is the screw ship-of-the-line *Re Galantuomo* (ex-*Monarca*), of the old Neapolitan Navy. She was launched in 1850.

Plate 22.

FS *Courbet*
Brest, France, 1886

The *Courbet* and her sister ship the *Dévastation* were the largest central-battery ironclads ever built, and they were almost the last. Extraordinary-looking ships, they bring to mind the inflated lines of modern nuclear-powered submarines.

French design doctrine called for pronounced ram bows and an exaggerated tumble home, the beam at the waterline being much greater than at the level of the upper deck. The armored redoubt was built out to the full waterline breadth of the ship, enabling guns placed behind ports or mounted on top of the battery to fire very nearly due forward and aft as well as on broadside bearings.

The principal armament comprised four 13.4-inch guns mounted in casemates at the diagonal corners of the battery. They were hydraulically operated but the emplacements were cramped and their rate of fire was slow. These guns were later replaced by 10.8-inch weapons, similar to those mounted at bow, stern, and on top of the battery on each side of the ship.

The armor belt was of wrought iron, up to fifteen inches thick, and extended for most of the length of the ship. There was a 2.4-inch armored deck level with the top of the belt, and the battery itself was armored to twenty feet above water level. *Courbet* had vertical compound engines driving twin screws and she could make 15.5 knots.

Courbet was laid down in 1875 but only completed eleven years later. She was taken out of service in 1910.

the Royal Navy's *Royal Sovereign* class, eight identical ships completed in 1892-1894. Tactically, there was much to be gained by the ability to deploy a group of ships with similar capabilities. The *Royal Sovereigns* were handsome ships with higher freeboard than the *Admirals*; they were considerably faster and they mounted bigger guns.

The new Chief Constructor of the Royal Navy, Sir William White, had been closely involved with the design of the *Admiral* class, and the new ships were entirely his responsibility. Nickel-alloy steel provided increased resistance to penetration, and triple-expansion engines gave better economy and performance. Their main armament was of 13.5-inch caliber and their secondary battery of ten six-inch guns was regarded as an important part of the ships' offensive power.

Big guns have a greater range than small ones. For a given muzzle velocity, the larger the caliber of a projectile the greater the distance it will carry, but in the 1880s useful range was limited by inaccuracy. Inconsistency in munitions and the lack of ranging equipment severely constrained the chances of making a hit at long range. The decisive phase of battle was therefore expected to take place at close quarters, less than a mile and a half, at which distance all sizes of gun could take effect. The quick-firers were expected to do great damage to the upperworks, while the big guns groped for a penetrating blow on the waterline which alone was capable of sinking an enemy ship.

Many nations found it necessary to equip their navies with ironclads. Throughout the nineteenth century France was by a large margin the second-ranking naval power, but Russia, Austria-Hungary, and Italy each built a force of seagoing ironclad warships to replace their wooden battle fleets. Spain, Turkey, Japan, China, and the three leading South American republics ordered ironclads for construction in foreign yards, and several smaller European countries such as Sweden, Denmark, and the Netherlands built units designed primarily, like the U.S. monitors, for harbor defense.

Prussia had only three seagoing ironclads in the navy at the time of going to war with France in 1870, but after the war she added more. In the last decade of the century the newly consolidated German Empire began to build up a substantial fleet of armored ships.

The United States was the last big country to take an interest in creating an armored fleet. It was not until 1886 that construction of battleships was authorized, and it was 1895 before the first two entered service. In the 1890s there was a swing of opinion away from isolationism, and public acceptance of the need for a strong modern navy. By the year 1900 a major building program was under way in the U.S.

The story of the ironclad concludes with what later came to be termed pre-Dreadnought battleships. The vessels built in the last years of the nineteenth century and in the early 1900s were precursors of the altogether more formidable armored ships which followed the appearance of the *Dreadnought* in 1906.

A new wire-wound twelve-inch gun had been developed by Armstrong, and smokeless propellant provided greater offensive power. The new guns were capable of throwing shells up to 12,000 yards, and efforts were made to improve the drilling of gun crews, estimating range, and adopting centralized fire control for correcting the aim. Telescopic sights were introduced in 1899, and the first range finder appeared three years later. These developments had a dramatic effect on the range of battle.

Pre-Dreadnought battleships were also better protected. Their armor was composed of Krupp face-hardened steel and their principal guns were again mounted in revolving turrets, these now being situated on the top of armored barbettes.

Around the turn of the century there was a tremendous burst of naval construction, reflecting rising political tensions between the major powers. But by 1906 all of these ships were rendered obsolescent by the advent of the first battleship armed exclusively with long-range guns.

[1] Tumble home means the amount by which the sides of a ship are sloped in towards the centerline above the maximum beam at the waterline.

Plate 23.

USS *Wampanoag*
Brooklyn Navy Yard, New York, 1874

Designed in response to the destruction caused by fast commerce raiders such as the *Alabama*, and with an eye to causing equal damage to British shipping in the event of war with that country, the *Wampanoag* achieved record speed on her trials.

Wampanoag was wooden built, unusually long for her beam, with the engine room set between the two boiler rooms giving rise to the distinctive spacing of her funnels. Her designed armament was ten nine-inch smooth-bores and three 60-pounder rifled guns and her top speed was a sensational seventeen knots, fastest in the world.

She was one of seven ships of slightly diverse designs that were laid down in 1863-1864, but she was not completed until 1867 and remained in commission for only three months. The ships became the subject of bitter controversy, centered around Isherwood, the engineer responsible for the design of their unorthodox geared propulsion machinery. It was said that their long narrow hulls lacked rigidity, that the engines were grossly uneconomical, and that there was insufficient provision for armament and stores. Some of the ships suffered from the wartime use of unseasoned timber.

Isherwood was hounded from office, and in the mood of post-war naval retrenchment the *Wampanoag* class was withdrawn from service.

LA GUERRE DE COURSE

Literally the phrase *la guerre de course* means "hunting warfare." Several nations concluded that the way to offset the preponderance of British power at sea would be by means of commerce raiding. No navy, however large, could be strong enough in all theaters simultaneously, and Confederate raiders like CSS *Alabama* during the American Civil War had shown how a handful of fast and enterprising cruisers could play havoc with worldwide mercantile trade.

The construction of USS *Wampanoag* and her sister ships by the U.S. Navy between 1863 and 1867 focused the attention of the British Admiralty. A class of large, fast, screw cruising warships was laid down in reply. They were iron-built but sheathed in teak and coppered to prevent fouling of the hulls in tropical waters.

For eighty years the prospect of commerce raiders set loose on trade routes remained the subject of serious concern in Whitehall. The threat materialized in 1914 and again in 1939. *Emden*, *Königsberg*, *Graf Spee*, and *Bismarck* each adopted the role of fox after the chickens, and each in turn was pursued by hounds. While Britain's ultimate command of the sea remained unshaken, and her worldwide network of bases existed to provide support, every hunt was bound to end in a kill. Winston Churchill, as First Lord of the Admiralty in 1914 during the four-month search for Admiral Graf von Spee's ships in the Pacific, described the raiders succinctly: "Like cut flowers," he said, "so fair to see, yet bound to die."

HMS *Shah*, one of the class of ships built to meet the threat represented by *Wampanoag*, never had occasion to fight an American ship. She was posted to the Pacific squadron and in 1877 was stationed off Peru. Rebels had taken possession of the principal unit in the Peruvian Navy, the ironclad *Huascar*. The government appealed to the Royal Navy to seize the renegade warship. The encounter was one of the few naval engagements experienced by the Royal Navy during a prolonged period of peace, and the outcome had an important influence on the design of future cruisers.

Huascar was an armored turret ship which had been built in England. *Shah*, which had no armor protection, was reluctant to come to close quarters and her guns were unable to make any impression on the rebel ironclad. *Huascar*, with her two ten-inch guns, failed to make a single hit on the British ship and so she eventually took refuge in port, surrendering to the authorities.

This incident called into question the effectiveness of large unarmored cruising ships. Attention was drawn to a new Russian warship, the *General Admiral*, which joined the fleet in 1875. She was smaller, slower, and less heavily armed than *Shah*, but she carried six-inch wrought iron armor. For this reason she has sometimes been described as the world's first armored cruiser.

Armored cruisers which took the form of small-scale broadside ironclads were built for the Royal Navy and the French during the 1870s. Sailing qualities were still considered important, but ships such as the *Northampton* were characterized by critics as too weak to stand up to battleships and yet too slow to run away.

The other direction of development after the *Shah* was a type of smaller, faster ship which was variously described as a second- or third-class cruiser, a protected cruiser, or a scout. Sir William Armstrong, the Tyneside shipbuilder and armaments manufacturer, predicted that the growing power of guns would be able to defeat any thickness of armor which could possibly be carried on a cruiser. He advocated building fast cruisers with no armor belt, a steel protective deck over the whole length of the ship, and a heavy armament of the new quick-firer medium-caliber guns. He was unable to convince the British Admiralty, but orders from Chile and China enabled the firm to proceed anyway with construction of ships along these lines.

The Chilean cruiser *Esmeralda* attracted widespread interest when she was delivered in 1884. She proved the fortune of the company, which received orders for fourteen "Elswick cruisers" from a number of foreign countries, and she undoubtedly had an influence on official opinion in Britain. The design of the *Apollo* class and subsequent second-class cruisers for the Royal Navy reflected Armstrong's ideas.

The elegant little *Apollo*s were completed in the early 1890s. They had a displacement of 3,400 tons, a top speed of twenty knots, and an armament of eight quick-firers and four torpedo tubes. Their protection, like the *Esmeralda*'s, consisted of a two-inch steel deck near water level below which lay the ships' engine rooms and magazines.

Two of the slim "Elswick cruisers" eventually found their way into the U.S. Navy. Ships under construction for Brazil, they were bought in the rush to expand the Navy during the Spanish-American War and were given the names USS *New Orleans* and *Albany*. Both cruisers gave long service and were not discarded until the 1920s.

In 1895, eleven years after *Esmeralda* was delivered to Chile, France completed construction of a bold new design of commerce raider. A long, slender vessel, she carried an armored belt of four-inch hardened steel from stem to stern. She was a striking-looking craft with a snout at the bow and

an almost equally long sloping stern. Widely spaced funnels were matched by tubular masts supporting two-tiered fighting tops. The ship was christened *Dupuy de Lôme*, after the designer of the first ironclad, *La Gloire*, and she was followed into service by a long succession of progressively larger and more formidable-looking armored cruisers.

Dupuy de Lôme had a top speed of twenty knots, unprecedented for an armored ship, and an armament of eight 7.6-inch and 6.4-inch guns, all mounted in individual turrets. As in other French designs, the armament was disposed in a diamond-shaped plan, with guns mounted in groups far forward, near the stern, and on either beam amidships. The hull was given exaggerated tumble home to provide the wing turrets with clear fields of fire fore and aft. Her displacement was 6,700 tons.

Armstrong's next design for the Chilean navy, the armored cruiser *O'Higgins*, was larger still at 8,500 tons, and she flaunted three tall, imposing funnels. Two of her eight-inch guns were mounted in turrets fore and aft and two more, plus ten six-inch guns, were mounted in armored casemates along the sides. She, too, started a vogue; four ships like her were supplied to Japan and she became the model for armored cruisers built for the U.S. and Britain.

In the last decade of the nineteenth century the pace of competition became furious. The Russians caused a stir with a ship called *Rurik*, also completed in 1895. She had a powerful armament and a heavy belt of armor, but compared with *Dupuy de Lôme* her design concept was quite old-fashioned. She went to sea first with barque rig and her armament was all arranged on the broadside. *Rurik* was closely followed by three more big armored cruisers, but they suffered badly at the hands of Japan's Armstrong-built cruisers at the Battle of Ulsan in 1904. *Rurik* was sunk and two others badly damaged.

The U.S. Navy also introduced cruisers designed for commerce raiding. USS *Columbia* and *Indianapolis*, completed in 1894, were fast, at twenty-one knots; they had a protective deck but only a relatively light armament. They were followed into service by USS *Olympia*, a slightly smaller ship with a heavier armament (fourteen eight-inch

Plate 24.

FS *Dupuy de Lôme*
la Grande Rade, Toulon, France, 1897

The armored cruiser *Dupuy de Lôme* caused a sensation with the novelty of her design. She had been conceived as a commerce raider at a period when war between France and Britain seemed a realistic possibility, but she was more than five years under construction and by the time of her completion in 1893 circumstances had changed.

Dupuy de Lôme is depicted against the backdrop of the fortified eminence of Mont Faron which dominates the roadstead of Toulon. On the right can be seen the newly-completed battleship *Charles Martel*.

The cruiser had a four-inch armored belt from stem to stern, backed by a protective deck and coal bunkers arranged over the engine and boiler rooms. She could make twenty knots, an unprecedented speed for an armored ship, and her armament of eight medium guns was mounted in electrically operated single-gun turrets.

The cutaway bow and stern were designed to avoid the effects of muzzle blast on deck.

Plate 25.

Amazonas and Almirante Barrozo
in the Tyne, Newcastle, England, 1897

The slim lines of the celebrated "Elswick cruiser" are shown to good effect in this view of two of them nearing completion for the Brazilian Navy. *Almirante Barrozo*, which is lying out in the stream, was the first to be delivered; she remained in service until 1948. Her sister ships *Amazonas* and *Almirante Abreu* were sold before delivery to the United States Navy, which found itself short of fast, modern warships at the outbreak of the Spanish-American War in 1898. The splendid gilded cartouche on the stern of *Amazonas* was modified to display at its center the Stars and Stripes and she was renamed USS *New Orleans*.

Designed by Sir Philip Watts, these cruisers were built by Armstrong at the company's new yard at Elswick, upstream from the city of Newcastle on the River Tyne. They were amongst the fastest cruisers of the day and they were the first to be armed with the new quick-firing six-inch guns. Their protection was limited to an armored deck near water level sloping down to join the sides of the ship, which provided four-inch-thick oblique armor over the engine and boiler rooms. The type was an export success, fourteen ships being sold to seven foreign navies, and the Royal Navy adopted more or less the same design, eight of which were built at Elswick.

In the background can be seen the high-level bridge spanning the Tyne in the center of Newcastle, with the red-painted swing bridge just visible beyond it. On the left is the grim keep of the medieval castle, and on the right lies the town of Gateshead.

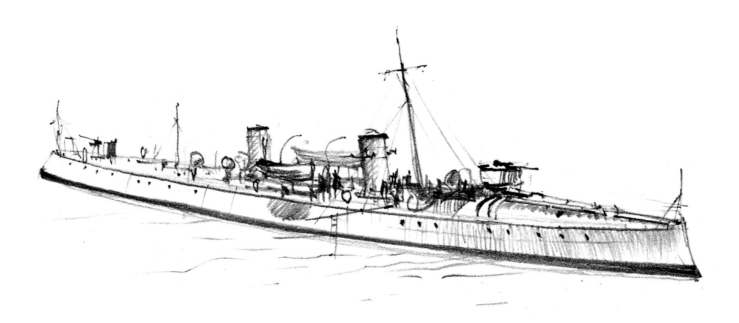

and five-inch guns). This was the ship that led Commodore George Dewey's successful attack on the Spanish at Manila Bay, and she is maintained in honor to this day in the Delaware River at Philadelphia. America, like France, then embarked on an ambitious program of armored cruiser construction which extended well into the new century.

The Royal Navy, confronting the prospect of marauders on vital shipping routes, built a force of large protected cruisers. Eleven ships of the *Blake* and *Edgar* classes were completed in 1892-1894. They carried two 9.2-inch guns, ten six-inch guns plus smaller weapons, and torpedo tubes. They were followed by two exceptional vessels—HMS *Powerful* and *Terrible*.

These last two ships were a direct response to the stationing of ships like *Rurik* at Vladivostok. The 14,000-ton cruisers were the longest warships of their day and exceeded the tonnage of most battleships. Their boiler rooms contained no less than forty-eight of the new watertube boilers, which were of course coal-fired, and their giant reciprocating engines produced 25,000 horsepower and drove them at twenty-two knots. Plants of this scale stretched stokehold crews to the limits of endurance: it was rumored on the lower deck that a third unit was to be built and that she would be known as HMS *Horrible*. Speed was

accompanied by great endurance.

Eventually the British, too, felt obliged to revert to building armored cruisers. Between 1900 and 1908 thirty-five were built, largely, it must be supposed, in order to counter the threat of commerce raiders.

During the Russo-Japanese War Admiral Heihachiro Togo made use of armored cruisers to augment the four battleships forming his battle line at Tsushima. They were lucky to escape loss, and their presence did much to cause an inflated view of an armored cruiser's worth. The arrival in 1908 of the all-big-gun Dreadnought cruiser, or "battle cruiser" as it came to be called, eclipsed the armored cruiser type completely.

So the cycle started by CSS *Alabama* reached its conclusion. The anticipated *guerre de course* failed to materialize in the nineteenth century. Few would have predicted the crushing naval defeat of Russia at the hands of Japan, and before the end of Queen Victoria's reign in 1901 Anglo-German antagonism was at no time a likely prospect. In the First World War German fast light cruisers and armed merchantmen proved to be the most dangerous and elusive commerce raiders, and fast light cruisers were what was needed to catch them.

Plate 26.

HMS *Andromache*, *Redwing*, and *Turquoise*
in the Old Harbour, Mombasa, 1890

The Weru Expedition of 1890 was not sufficiently important to have found a place in history books. The story is recorded in a framed sheet of yellowed writing paper which hangs in an inconspicuous passage at the Mombasa Club.

A German missionary was murdered by natives in a village near Gedi, on the coast between Mombasa and Malindi. The German foreign office called upon Britain, which administered a protectorate over the Sultan of Zanzibar's mainland dominion, to enforce law and order.

A third-class protected cruiser, a screw sloop, and a gunboat were sent up the coast from Mombasa, two brass cannon were landed together with a detachment of marines, and those responsible for the crime were brought to book.

The three warships are depicted in the Old Harbour at Mombasa, together with lateen-rigged dhows from the Persian Gulf which are busy loading cargo in the steamy equatorial heat.

On the left is the newly built cruiser HMS *Andromache*, a representative of the delicate, yacht-like ships of the *Apollo* class. On the right is HMS *Redwing*, a typical late-Victorian gunboat of composite construction with barquentine rig, and in the background a wooden screw corvette called HMS *Turquoise*, sister ship of the more famous *Calliope*.

Plate 27.

SMS *Königsberg*
Dar es Salaam, German East Africa, 1914

On 6 June 1914, the light cruiser
SMS *Königsberg* arrived at Dar es Salaam,
the capital of German East Africa. She
was there to take part in celebrations to
mark the completion of the railroad to
Kigoma on Lake Tanganyika, 800 miles to
the west. The Kaiser was due to visit the
colony early in August.

The cruiser is portrayed in the lovely
landlocked harbor of Dar es Salaam. The
Governor has just landed at his private
jetty and is about to inspect a small guard
of honor of askaris. On the right is the
Resident Magistrate's Court, one of a
number of handsome German public
buildings that still survive.

The Kaiser's visit never took place.
Other events unfolded in Europe in July
1914. The *Königsberg* was ordered to
engage as a commerce raider in "la guerre
de course." She was not very successful,
but achieved one brief moment of glory
when she found and sank the British
cruiser *Pegasus* which had been lying
under repair at Zanzibar.

Withdrawing from this exploit the
Königsberg herself suffered an engine
breakdown and was obliged to take refuge
in the delta of the Rufiji River. After
months of search, followed by fruitless
attempts to reach her in her jungle
hideout, the Royal Navy finally sent two
shallow-draft river monitors into the
mouth of the Rufiji. They sank the
Königsberg by indirect fire over interven-
ing tree-clad islands, the fall of shot being
directed for the first time by aircraft.

Outside the entrance to Fort Jesus in
Mombasa can be seen one of the
Königsberg's guns mounted as a trophy,
together with one rescued from the
sunken *Pegasus*. The two artillery pieces
were amongst those fished out of the
water and put to further use by both sides
in the land campaign between 1914 and
1918.

Plate 28.

USS *Olympia*
Hong Kong, 1898

Commodore George Dewey's flagship, the protected cruiser USS *Olympia*, was at Hong Kong in February 1898 at the outbreak of the Spanish-American War. She is seen moored off the Royal Navy dockyard, the graceful Victorian buildings of which appear in the background. Note the massive sheerlegs on the quay which were used in those days for hoisting heavy items.

The *Olympia* sailed with the rest of the U.S. East Asiatic Squadron for the Spanish colony of the Philippines. Dewey's four cruisers and two gunboats were more than a match for the seven elderly warships at Manila under command of Admiral Montojo. The Spanish warships lay at anchor under the protection of the guns of Cavite, but all seven were sunk by Dewey's force without casualty to the Americans.

The *Olympia* is still afloat, moored in the Delaware close to the foot of Market Street in downtown Philadelphia. One can climb down into the engine rooms, one of the few places where an example of the once-universal, enormous triple-expansion reciprocating engines can still be seen. In November 1992 the *Olympia* celebrated the centenary of her launch from the Union Iron Works at San Francisco.

COCHRANE

It was in 1792 that the revolutionary regime in France was taken over by the mob. The storming of the Tuileries was succeeded by the massacre of the Swiss Guard and the Reign of Terror. Reports of 11,000 lives lost in August horrified public opinion in Britain, which had hitherto been benevolent towards the spirit of reform. In January 1793, King Louis XVI and Marie Antoinette were put to the guillotine, and the next month France declared war on England and Holland.

So commenced a period of twenty-two years of almost continuous hostilities between Britain and France, a war to contain the French attempt at domination of Europe, including the British Isles, and latterly to oppose the tyranny of Napoleon Bonaparte, self-proclaimed Emperor of the French.

Britain's allies waxed and waned throughout nearly a quarter of a century of fighting. Campaigns swung to and fro across Europe, rolling as far as the pyramids of Egypt and the gates of Moscow in the east, and stopping short only at the lines of Torres Vedras before Lisbon in the west. The constant factor was the command of the sea which was never relaxed by the Royal Navy, and the limitation imposed on French strategy by the continental blockade.

In the first year of the Napoleonic Wars, Thomas Cochrane entered the Navy at the age of eighteen. Lord Cochrane, as he was known, was the courtesy title of the eldest son of the Earl of Dundonald. His father died in 1838, whereupon Cochrane became the tenth Earl.[1]

The Royal Navy was a well-honed instrument of power with intercontinental reach, but it was at the same time riddled with abuses which the next century would find preposterous. Rank was conferred often on the basis of privilege, many commanding officers abused their powers, and gross peculation was practiced at the Admiralty and in the dockyards. Most particularly, the system of prize courts was steeped in fraud, which led to injustice in the distribution of proceeds from the capture of enemy ships. The sums involved were very large, and prize money was a vital consideration in a naval officer's career.

Cochrane tackled his duties with skillful seamanship, enthusiasm, and what must have been an infectious gaiety. He displayed also a spirit of independence that occasionally strayed into insubordination.

In 1800 the inexperienced lieutenant was fortunate to secure an early command, the tiny sloop *Speedy*. Her armament was so puny that an entire broadside of pellets from her 4-pounders would fit into a pocket. Nonetheless Cochrane worked to ensure that his crew was trained to a hairsbreadth in gunnery and seamanship, and he held them under instant discipline. At the age of twenty-five he captured his first prize and began to demonstrate his valor.

His first triumph was the capture of the 32-gun Spanish frigate *Gamo*. He brought his little sloop so close under the hull of the frigate that she was unable to depress her guns sufficiently to bring them to bear. Boarding the enemy ship at the head of his crew, Cochrane and his men overwhelmed six times their number of Spaniards. The collapse of the defense was hastened by the action of one of

HMS Ringdove 1882

Cochrane's seamen, who had been detailed ahead of time to haul down the Spanish colors. Success was partly due to the sheer effrontery of the maneuver: no frigate captain would anticipate being boarded by so inferior an antagonist.

The prize court failed to reward *Speedy*'s crew, and Cochrane himself was denied promotion. Quick to take offense, he made himself unpopular by repeated requests for recognition and reward, eventually infuriating the First Lord of the Admiralty, Lord St. Vincent.

Throughout his career Cochrane was resolute in exposing injustices, real or supposed, and consequently he was seen by the official mind as constantly causing trouble. As a result he stirred up a large body of resentment amongst senior officers and men of political influence.

In the course of a year *Speedy* captured more than fifty vessels and 534 prisoners. Cochrane's escapades terminated in an heroic action against three French line-of-battle ships, at the end of which he was obliged to capitulate. In a gesture of respect for his gallantry the French captain declined to accept Cochrane's proffered sword. He remained a prisoner for only a couple of weeks before being freed in exchange for a French officer.

The Peace of Amiens in 1801 brought a pause in hostilities between England and France which lasted less than eighteen months. Britain grew increasingly alarmed, however, at evidence of preparations for an invasion, and Bonaparte raged at the British ambassador over the British retention of a naval base in Malta. He announced that England must choose to join him or be crushed, and he promised to lead the invasion himself.

Warfare resumed in 1803, and plans were put in hand to counterattack any French beachheads which might be established in England and to move the seat of government from London. Lord St. Vincent was nevertheless slow to appoint Cochrane to a new command. When he did, the ship was an old collier which was in a state of decay bordering on unseaworthiness.

Cochrane's assignment to HMS *Arab* was a rebuke. For fifteen months he was obliged to patrol the empty seas north of Scotland in a vessel that, he said, "sailed like a haystack."

Fortunately for Cochrane a change of government brought William Pitt the Younger back to power as Prime Minister. St. Vincent was replaced as First Lord by Viscount Melville, who did not share St. Vincent's opinion of Cochrane as "mad, romantic, money-getting and not truth-telling."

Cochrane was appointed to a new thirty-two-gun frigate called the *Pallas*. Sailing from Plymouth in January 1805, *Pallas* took part in the Spanish blockade, amassing a fortune in captured merchant vessels. Cochrane, now promoted to post-captain, demonstrated that quality of impudence coupled with the power of rapid improvisation that was to bring frequent success in action.

On one occasion *Pallas* was encountered by three French line-of-battle ships. A storm was rising, and the pursuing ships were prevented from using their guns effectively until they could come alongside their victim. Bracing the frigate's masts with extra hawsers, Cochrane piled on every scrap of canvas and drove his ship through heavy seas. The larger men-of-war were still gaining, however, with their greater spread of canvas taut under what had now developed into a full gale. As his ship was about to be overhauled, Cochrane sent the crew aloft and at a signal dropped every sail at the same moment. With the helm hard over the frigate was suddenly brought up, shaking from stem to stern, and the French ships-of-the-line careered past in a welter of white water.

It took the Frenchmen so long to shorten sail and to trim to the new tack that *Pallas* was well ahead by nightfall.

Throughout the hours of darkness the French pursued the dim glow of light coming from the English frigate. At dawn they found that they had been following a ballasted cask on which was mounted a lantern. Of *Pallas* there was no sign.

In June 1805 Cochrane obtained leave of absence from the Navy to stand for election to Parliament. He stood as a Radical, in opposition to the governing Tories and in favor of parliamentary reform. The electoral system was far from providing fair representation: it was a maze of anomalies and inconsistencies which served those in power, and those with the means and the influence to buy it. Cochrane chose the most corrupt electoral district in England, one where so few people were entitled to vote that the seat was customarily bought by the highest bidder.

Refusing to buy votes, he naturally failed in the first election, but afterwards he offered a "reward" to the few who had cast a vote for him. The reward was a larger sum than had been paid to those who had voted for the successful candidate.

Another general election took place twelve months later and Cochrane duly won the seat, but to the chagrin of the voters he paid no rewards.

In October 1805, Admiral Lord Nelson, with the principal British fleet, finally brought to action and decisively defeated the great combined Spanish and French fleet which had been assembled to bring about the invasion of England. The battle, which took place off Cadiz, was named for Cape Trafalgar.

In the meantime *Pallas* was back in action in the Bay of Biscay. She carried on board a special eighteen-oared galley, designed and built by Cochrane at his own expense. Cochrane made good use of this vessel in boarding French merchantmen up and down the coast. The reputation of *Pallas* preceded her, and merchantmen were run aground and abandoned at the mere sight of the approaching frigate.

In a nighttime foray in the mouth of the Gironde, downstream from Bordeaux, Cochrane's men boarded and captured the duty guard ship. By daylight three French corvettes were seen converging on *Pallas*, which had been largely denuded of her crew. The frigate nevertheless set sail instantly, menaced the first of the corvettes so that she fled and went aground, and then pursued the others one by one onto sandbanks. Cochrane's reputation reached the ears of Napoleon himself.

His next appointment was to command the thirty-eight-gun frigate *Imperieuse*. He continued his buccaneering activities off the French coast, audaciously landing marines to destroy the shore defenses at Arcachon, for instance, as a prelude to setting ablaze a convoy of seven ships under the guns of the fort. *Imperieuse* was then ordered to the Mediterranean.

Cochrane's operations were a blend of daring and practical joke. He used subterfuge (flying false colors before actually opening fire was considered a legitimate ruse of war) and he was always careful to incur no avoidable casualties. He excelled in the game of landing parties on a hostile coast to lay booby-traps and to spike the guns of coastal batteries. In one action he swung brass cannon from a cliff to the deck of his frigate by means of tackle and capstan.

Imperieuse demoralized the military garrison of Port Vendre by a well-judged combination of feinting to draw off the troops, then landing a party of marines behind the enemy to lay explosives. Subsequently a close-range broadside demolished an exposed section of cliff road while cavalry was racing back along it to defend the port.

Cochrane adopted the habit of replenishing his ship by sailing up the River Rhône into French territory until she reached fresh water to pump aboard, and taking fresh meat on the hoof.

The climax of these incursions was Cochrane's defense of Rosas, a small town near the Spanish border with France. He was under orders to assist Spanish guerrillas in delaying a column of 6,000 French troops marching into Spain.

Cochrane landed eighty sailors and took possession of an old coastal fort. For two weeks, and with the loss of only three men, he held up the French regular infantry supported by five batteries of 24-pounder cannon. He succeeded because he well understood the limitations of artillery and anticipated the area of wall which would be the most likely target to effect a breach. A slippery pitfall was rigged up inside the walls, seeded with mines.

The defenders made elaborate use of explosive devices. At the end the landing party was evacuated to *Imperieuse* by means of lines dropped over the edge of the cliff. The fort was demolished in one mighty delayed explosion timed to go off when the jubilant attacking troops had swarmed inside.

Cochrane was honored on his return from the Mediterranean with the award of a knighthood. He advocated pursuing amphibious warfare on the Atlantic coast of France. In his view a small force would be able to take possession of the offshore islands in the Bay of Biscay, and the presence of such a force would cripple coastwise shipping and divert substantial French forces to coast defense. In this way, he thought, the long and costly campaign conducted by Wellington against Napoleon's armies in Portugal and Spain might have been avoided.

At this moment the British blockade was breached. In 1809 ships under the command of Admiral Lord Gambier were blown off station outside the port of Brest by a gale, and the French squadron emerged to join forces with ships from Lorient and arrived in strength at the anchorage of Basque Roads. The combined fleet of eleven ships-of-the-line plus frigates was there being prepared to sail for Martinique. So serious was this threat that Gambier was ordered to attack the French without delay. The roadstead was well protected by islands mounting coastal batteries, between which the French had erected a formidable floating boom, and there were shoals the extent of which the British admiral was uncertain.

Cochrane, with his recent knowledge of operations in these coastal waters, was recalled to the Admiralty and asked to assist with the assault. He was not keen to be brought in ahead of many more senior officers already with Gambier's fleet, because of the inevitable jealousy that this would cause. Eventually he was ordered by the Admiralty to lead the attack. ("He is ruthless enough to try," the Admiralty minutes recorded, "and will serve as a useful scapegoat

Plate 29.

USS *Maine*

passing Castillo del Morro, Havana, Cuba, 1898

On January 25, 1898, the new battleship USS *Maine* steamed into Havana on a courtesy visit. In the foreground are citizens who have come to watch the spectacle from the Malecón, opposite the end of the Paseo del Prado. Note the Spanish flag flying above the old fortress of the Castillo del Morro in the background.

Three weeks later the American battleship blew up at her moorings in the harbor with the loss of two-thirds of her crew. Anti-Spanish sentiment in the United States was inflamed, and a U.S. Navy court of inquiry blamed the disaster on the explosion of a mine placed under the hull. The incident became a factor which led to the outbreak of the Spanish-American War.

Research in recent years indicates that the explosion was internal, which suggests that the cause is likely to have been accidental. It was possibly due to chemical deterioration of propellant

powder, which brought about the loss of a number of warships in the period. Another possibility is spontaneous combustion in a coal bunker adjoining one of the magazines, a hazard which had been detected on board on an earlier occasion.

The *Maine* was the first U.S. ironclad designed for oceangoing service since the USS *New Ironsides*, and the first battleship commissioned in the U.S. Navy.

if the project fails.")

Cochrane concocted a plan to ram the boom by night with vessels filled with explosives, followed by fire ships which would be taken through the resulting gaps in the defense.

The scheme worked perfectly. It was a dark night. There was a two-mile width of channel between the shoals, and the three explosive-filled craft surged in with a strong northwest wind behind the flood tide.

Cochrane himself was the last to leave his craft, abandoning her minutes before she struck the boom. The vessel, packed with 1,500 barrels of powder, erupted in a mighty explosion. A second explosive craft breached the boom. French patrolling boats were swamped in the ensuing detonation.

Four Royal Navy frigates moved in behind the explosion to guide fire ships through the gaps. As the French began to make out the dark shapes of fire ships gliding into their crowded anchorage, they assumed that they carried more explosive devices and hastily slipped their cables. The tide began to turn, and one after another the French men-of-war went aground. Daylight revealed nine line-of-battle ships stranded on sandbanks. As the tide ebbed, the ships heeled over, leaving their bottoms exposed helplessly to enemy gunfire.

Cochrane urgently signaled Gambier advising him of the French predicament, but the admiral lingered, being reluctant to bring his line-of-battle ships into the uncertain waters of the channel. The two remaining French liners ran aground. Cochrane could still get no move out of Gambier; neither could he get permission to go in on his own. Finally, beside himself with impatience at the lost opportunity, Cochrane allowed *Imperieuse* to drift amongst the French and thus to become engaged.

Cochrane's ship at last received some help from the nearer British frigates, and throughout the night a mêlée took place in the constricted anchorage. Three French liners surrendered to the *Imperieuse* and her consorts and another was burnt by her crew to avoid capture.

In the light of dawn Admiral Gambier ordered Cochrane to break off the action and rejoin the main body of the fleet at sea, so he was obliged to leave the roadstead without completing the destruction of the enemy. Nevertheless the engagement was seen as a significant success.

When they met, Gambier praised Cochrane for his gallantry, but Cochrane reproached the admiral for his failure to come to the support of the frigates and tried to persuade him even then to renew the action. Gambier, however, ordered Cochrane back to England, and his dispatches omitted all reference to Cochrane's role in the battle.

The beleaguered Tory government decided to make some political capital out of success by moving a vote of thanks to Gambier in the House of Commons. Cochrane, in his capacity as a Member of Parliament, impertinently opposed the motion. The wrangle began to attract public attention.

Gambier was incensed and called for a court-martial to clear his reputation. Under the circumstances the proceedings were stage-managed to ensure the vindication of the Commander in Chief and the government. Evidence was withheld, spurious charts were introduced as evidence, and Cochrane was prevented from giving his own account of the events.

In the end Gambier was cleared, and the House of Commons duly passed the motion of thanks. The Admiralty refused to give Cochrane another command at sea.

Cochrane's injudicious behavior, his attacks on mismanagement at the Admiralty, and his impetuous support for one of the wildest Radical members of Parliament made him a large number of enemies.

There is little doubt that he was framed. In 1814 a scandal occurred involving fraudulent speculation on the stock exchange. Cochrane's uncle seems to have been responsible for employing an army officer to arrive in London with a false report of the defeat of French armies and the death of Napoleon. This caused the price of stock to soar and allowed him to reap large profits.

The spurious messenger was found to have called at Cochrane's house for a change of clothes, and Cochrane was charged with fraud, jointly with his uncle and an accomplice. The two conspirators fled the country and Cochrane was left alone to face trial. There is reason to believe that at least one witness gave perjured evidence. Cochrane's defense was bungled and he was fined, condemned to four months in prison, ignominiously discharged from the Navy, and stripped of his knighthood.

Convinced that his imprisonment was not only unjust but illegal, he climbed over rooftops and leaped from a high wall to escape from gaol. One week later Cochrane calmly made his appearance in the House of Commons. He claimed parliamentary immunity and had to be forcibly removed from the chamber.

When he had completed his term in prison (his fine having been paid by popular subscription in his parliamentary constituency), Cochrane returned to the House of Commons. There he introduced a motion to impeach the Lord Chief Justice on charges of misrepresentation, partiality, and injustice. Needless to say the motion was rejected.

A few months later the seemingly endless war with France was finally brought to an end by conclusive victory at Waterloo.

In the period of post-war unemployment Cochrane threw himself deeply into Radical politics. He campaigned for reform of the electoral system and fought implacably against sinecure (reward for political services by means of a lucrative appointment without duties to perform).

The next phase of Cochrane's career was devoted to the cause of nationhood and democracy in South America and in Greece.

In Chile, command of the sea had enabled Spain to maintain garrisons up and down the coast in the face of widespread popular insurrection. Cochrane was recruited by the revolutionary government to form and command a Chilean navy, and his first act was to arrange the start of construction of a steam warship in London. In 1817 he went ahead to South America, where his arrival in Santiago was greeted with enthusiasm.

His greatest coup was the capture of the Spanish frigate *Esmeralda*, and this exploit acquired the character of

legend. The forty-four-gun man-of-war was the largest and strongest unit in the Spanish Pacific squadron, and her loss turned out to be the death blow to Spanish power on the west coast.

Esmeralda lay in the fortified harbor of Callao, the port of Lima, in which were present also the U.S. frigate *Macedonian* and the British *Hyperion*. Cochrane went in by night with fourteen small boats. They were challenged by one of the Spanish guard ships, but he brought his own boat softly alongside her and quietly subdued the captain. Cochrane's men boarded the frigate simultaneously from two sides, and though he was wounded his crew rapidly took possession of the ship.

The most adroit stroke was to hoist in *Esmeralda's* rigging three lanterns corresponding to the signal lights that he observed were being carried by the American and British ships. As the neutral vessels hastily got under way to avoid becoming embroiled in the fight, Cochrane slipped past the Spanish shore batteries masquerading as one of them.

The reputation of the Scottish admiral soared. Little more exertion was needed to overawe the remaining Spanish ships and garrisons, and independent republics were established in both Chile and Peru. Cochrane was

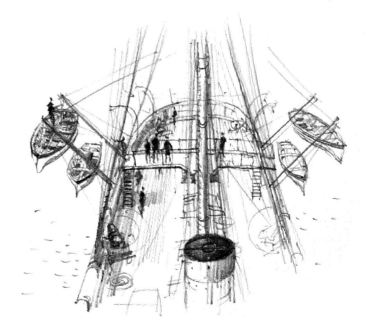

bitterly disappointed at the tyrannical behavior of San Martin, and at the shabby treatment he himself received at the hands of the new government after victory had been accomplished. He left Valparaiso with this proclamation.

Chileños, my fellow countrymen. You know that independence is purchased at the point of the bayonet. Know also that Liberty is founded on good faith, and on the laws of honour, and that those who infringe upon these are your only enemies, amongst whom you will never find Cochrane.

Brazil was the next nation to solicit Cochrane's services. The King of Portugal had fled to the colony when Napoleon's troops overran his country, and on his return to Lisbon he left his son Dom Pedro as regent of Brazil. In 1822 Dom Pedro put himself at the head of a popular movement for independence from Portugal.

The military situation was the same as on the west coast. So long as Portugal retained command of the sea it could control the country through a dozen garrisons. Only around Rio de Janeiro in the south could the new regime establish some sort of autonomous region.

Cochrane could only find enough reliable seamen, mostly Europeans and Americans, to man one ship, the seventy-four-gun ship-of-the-line *Pedro Primiero*. The rest of his little squadron was of doubtful fighting value.

Ostentatiously Cochrane prepared fire ships. Approaching the Portuguese stronghold of Bahia at night, he penetrated the harbor with his flagship disguised as an English merchantman. When the truth dawned on the governor, he was so alarmed that Cochrane had been so close and was so afraid of the prospect of fire ships in the confined anchorage that he ordered immediate evacuation.

The Portuguese convoy that set out from Bahia for Maranham to the north included seventy transports. One by one Cochrane picked them off. Captured ships were dismasted, leaving them no option but to drift back to the coast, now in rebel hands.

Pedro Primiero outstripped and outmaneuvered the Portuguese men-of-war. Cochrane drew off the escort in pursuit while the rest of his squadron dealt with the merchant vessels at their leisure.

Breaking off his attacks, Cochrane headed straight for the port of Maranham. He skirted the slow-moving Portuguese fleet, arriving twenty-four hours ahead of his quarry. *Pedro Primiero* sailed boldly into harbor flying the Portuguese colors. The commandant, anticipating the arrival of reinforcements from Bahia, sent out a brig to congratulate the captain on his safe arrival.

Cochrane greeted the Portuguese officer on behalf of the rebel regime in Rio. He then informed the commandant that the fleet arriving the following morning was not Portuguese at all. He said that an invasion force was approaching, filled with revolutionary troops who would be hard to restrain from plunder and retribution.

The Portuguese commandant jumped eagerly at Cochrane's offer of negotiation. Senior officials swore allegiance to the new regime of Brazil and the fortifications were surrendered.

When the Portuguese ships finally sighted the harbor forts they saw not the Portuguese flag but Brazilian colors. Denied refuge in Maranham, the remnants of the Portuguese colonial forces made their weary way across the Atlantic back to their homeland.

Cochrane's services to the new government of Brazil concluded in a wrangle over his salary and prize money. The country was split into successive warring factions, and he valiantly tried to support the authority of the central government headed by Dom Pedro I. After six months he resigned and returned home. In Scotland, at least, he received a hero's welcome.

The year was 1825. Rebellion had broken out against Turkish rule in Greece. The vision of democracy and the idealism of ancient Athens appealed to the imagination of liberal England. The poetry of Shelley and the example of Lord Byron expressed British attachment to the glory of the Hellenic dream.

Cochrane took more practical steps to support the cause. He played a role in helping to raise two substantial loans on the London market, and he consented to accept command of the Greek Navy. The Greeks also appointed an Englishman to command the army, and the British

Plate 30.

Pelayo
Port Said, Egypt, 1898

At the outbreak of the Spanish-American War the Spanish Navy assembled a squadron under the command of Admiral Camara with his flag in the battleship *Pelayo*. The force included the two modern cruisers, *Carlos V* and *Alfonso XII*, and six brand-new destroyers built in Britain. The Navy also acquired ten fast transatlantic liners as armed merchant cruisers and troop transports.

With news of Admiral Montojo's defeat at the Battle of Manila Bay this force was given orders to proceed to the Philippines. No sooner had the ships passed through the Suez Canal than word was received of the loss of the Spanish squadron at Santiago Bay in Cuba, which put the coast of Spain itself at risk of attack by the U.S. Navy. Camara was therefore ordered to return, and ships of his squadron are here portrayed lying at Port Said on their way back into the Mediterranean on 11 July 1898. The war ended in August.

The *Pelayo*, the most powerful ship in the Spanish Navy, was built in France between 1885 and 1890. She had a displacement of 10,000 tons, mounted two 12.5-inch guns, two 11-inch, twelve 4.7-inch, and seven torpedo tubes. She was heavily armored, the main belt being composed of eighteen-inch-thick Creusot steel.

Admiral Camara's squadron was far stronger and more up-to-date than either of the two which saw combat with the U.S. Navy in the Philippines and at Cuba.

government went so far as to seek support from Russia and France for recognition of the right of Greece to independence.

Cochrane ordered six steam-powered warships in London, and in New York two of the "heavy" sixty-gun frigates which had become a specialty of the U.S. Navy.

His experiences in the first few months of fighting in Greece were not encouraging. The Greeks kept splitting into factions under rival leaders, and the campaign to recapture the Acropolis at Athens failed due to the indiscipline of Greek troops. The Greek Army was described by one British observer as "generally speaking a mob; and a commander can only count on keeping it together as long as there is prospect of plunder without danger."

The Turkish forces were being assisted by the Egyptian Navy. Cochrane therefore took the first of his new frigates, together with some smaller warships, to raid the Egyptian port of Alexandria. The crews proved unreliable and little was achieved. However, the first of the steamers, *Karteria*, achieved some modest success under Captain Hastings in the Gulf of Lepanto.

Turkish resistance to Greek independence was brought to an abrupt end by the Battle of Navarino. There, allied naval forces under the command of the British Admiral Sir Edward Codrington were blockading the Turko-Egyptian fleet, attempting to enforce an armistice aimed at restoring peace, when one of the Turkish gunners fired the first shot.

The outcome was a massacre. The allied fleet with ten British line-of-battle ships, eight Russian, and seven French devastated the fleet of eighty-two Turkish warships. The concerted firepower of the western men-of-war caused terrible destruction: fifty Turkish ships were burned or demolished by explosions and some 6,000 men lost their lives.

This was the last naval battle to take place in the age of sail.

In 1830, thirteen years after he had left for Chile, Cochrane returned to a very different England. Parliament was seething with debate leading to final passage of the Reform Bill, and Cochrane's record seemed the embodiment of enlightenment in the political climate of the time.

On the death of his father Cochrane became the Earl of Dundonald, thus gaining a seat in the House of Lords. The government finally agreed to review his case, and he was granted a free pardon. Thereafter he was restored to the Navy list with the rank of Rear Admiral.

With the accession of Queen Victoria in 1837 the deeds and the attitudes of the Georgian era began to be seen in a very different light. Cochrane was perceived in the role of a hero who had championed the cause of freedom abroad and reform at home. He had outlived most of his old enemies, and the young Queen learned of his exploits and conceived an admiration for the old admiral.

In 1847 Cochrane was restored to his knighthood in the Order of the Bath, and the next year he hoisted his flag as Commander in Chief of the America and West Indies Station.

It was during this tour of duty that he became acquainted with the famous Pitch Lake in Trinidad, the world's only source of natural asphalt. He had inherited from his father a scientific interest in the family's coal mines at Culross in Fife. Byproducts of coal tar were used for caulking, for street lighting, and for paving roads. He explored possibilities in the use of natural asphalt for constructing sewers, as fuel for steamships, and as electrical insulation.

Before his trial and conviction in 1813 Cochrane had put forward to the Prince Regent elaborate plans for weapons based on the use of chemicals. His two main ideas were for the saturation bombardment of the French invasion ports by what he termed "temporary mortars," and for gas attack. The "temporary mortars" would be hulks filled with clay on which was bedded a layer of gunpowder, shells, and rockets, packed down with chains. They were to be moored by night close outside an enemy harbor and ballasted so that they would list towards the target. Three such hulks could bombard an area half a mile square with 6,000 shells.

He advocated gas attack by "sulphur ships." Charcoal

would be laid above a ballast of clay, with sulphur compound on top. When ignited this mixture would produce a poisonous gas which would drive troops out of shore defenses.

Experiments were conducted by Cochrane on his own account in the Mediterranean, but although his ideas were given some credibility, he had made himself so unpopular over the Gambier affair that the matter was not taken up.

Cochrane also devoted much attention to the development of steamships. He took out patents for a rotary steam engine and for a type of propeller, and he built an experimental steamboat on the Thames. He advocated the use of auxiliary steam power for line-of-battle ships and the employment of small, fast steamers armed with a single heavy gun.

He was responsible for getting the Navy to proceed with construction of the steam frigate *Janus* in 1845. The ship was to be powered by a rotary engine of American design but it was not a success. Interestingly, she was a "double-ender," an arrangement which saw widespread use in the American Civil War seventeen years later.

In 1854 Britain and France went to war with Russia over the Russian occupation of Balkan Turkey. Cochrane asked for a command, and he pressed forward his ideas for the use of unconventional means of warfare. He made detailed proposals for the reduction of the forts at Sevastopol and at Kronstadt near St. Petersburg, making

use of "sulphur ships," close-range "temporary mortars," and of naphtha floated on the surface of the sea and ignited by means of potassium. He also proposed the use of chemicals for generating smoke screens to cover the landing of troops on defended positions.

The proposed use of "noxious weapons" gave cause for official hesitation not only because of the likelihood of retaliation, but also because they seemed ungallant in a world which had not yet descended to unrestricted means of warfare. Nevertheless towards the end of the bitter Crimean campaign, when casualties had mounted beyond imagination, there were serious thoughts about putting such measures into practice. There was even a move in Parliament to put Cochrane in command of an independent operation. But the war came to an end before these plans materialized.

Cochrane died in 1860, and he was accorded the supreme national honor of a tomb in Westminster Abbey. One year after his death his third son, Arthur Cochrane, was appointed captain of HMS *Warrior*, the world's first iron-built battleship. A keen young officer joined the ship as gunnery lieutenant in 1863; his name was John Arbuthnot Fisher.

[1] English peers have the right to sit in the House of Lords. Only a limited number of Scottish peers — the Representative Peers — have the right to do so, and they included the Earl of Dundonald. Other Scottish peers and the sons of peers can stand for election to the House of Commons.

Plate 31.

HMS *Inflexible*
Alexandria, Egypt, 1882

Jackie Fisher was associated during his career with three technically adventurous ships. The second of these was an ironclad called HMS *Inflexible* which was completed in 1880. Fisher was her first captain.

Bred out of the growing competition between bigger guns and thicker armor, she had an armored deck below water level in place of the usual armored belt, surmounted by what was termed a "cita-del" faced with armor of immense thickness supporting two massive turrets equipped with giant guns.

Initially, she was received with acclaim. Her sixteen-inch guns were capable, in theory, of demolishing just about anything which could float. They were, however, muzzle-loading rifles, and since they were too long to retract into the turret they had to be loaded by depressing the barrels below a certain part of the armored deck. Only one gun could be discharged at a time, for fear of damaging the structure of the ship. Her rate of fire was therefore, one might say, deliberate.

Inflexible went into action at the bombardment of Alexandria, in 1882, where naval gunfire directed at stone fortifications turned out to be disconcertingly inaccurate. The attack caused the forts to be abandoned, but on inspection the damage proved to be far from commensurate with the weight of the bombardment.

The ironclad is depicted after the battle, lying at moorings in the harbor at Alexandria with both turrets trained to port. Note the broad beam and narrow superstructure, designed to afford both turrets the widest possible field of fire.

FISHER

Jackie Fisher operated in a very different world from Lord Cochrane's. In personality the two evidently had much in common. They were both ambitious and forceful characters. They were proficient sailors; each had a burning interest in improving the Navy, its administration, and its methods of warfare. Both men had imagination and foresight which enabled them to anticipate the weapons and the technology of future naval warfare. They were idealists, they shared the gift of being able to charm as well as to arouse antagonism, and they both inspired loyalty and affection on the lower deck.

But their careers followed very different paths. As a young midshipman Fisher took part in a desperate landing operation in China in 1859. At Alexandria in 1882 he led a naval party ashore which attracted popular attention by overawing far superior military forces with the help of a makeshift armored train. But after this escapade he saw no more action; his battles would be fought in the corridors of power.

Fisher's family background provided him with no advantages, socially or financially. From the very beginning of his career, however, his enthusiasm, his high spirits, and most importantly, perhaps, his winning manner, gained him the support of senior officers under whom he served. He enjoyed the benefit of unashamed favoritism and he himself, in later years, was as generous in his favors as he was intolerant of those whom he regarded as obstructive. Officers who were fired by his enthusiasm were said "to have swum into the fishpond," but he provoked opposition by his impatience and by the vehemence with which he hammered through his ideas.

Fisher entered the Navy in 1854. His initial assignment was to HMS *Victory*, the wooden three-decker which had been Nelson's flagship at Trafalgar. This historic ship was, and remains to this day, the flagship of the Port Admiral at Portsmouth. In 1854 *Victory* was nearly 100 years old, but she was still an active fighting unit.

Fisher's career was implicated with three revolutionary warships, *Warrior*, *Inflexible*, and *Dreadnought*. After service on the China Station he was appointed as gunnery lieutenant of the Navy's first ironclad, HMS *Warrior*. She was the crack ship in the Navy, focus of public attention and the subject of visits by foreign dignitaries and senior naval officers. Fisher's dedication to the improvement of gunnery technique was demonstrated before an attentive audience.

From this job he went on to the Navy's gunnery school in HMS *Excellent*, where he was put in charge of torpedo instruction. After another spell in the Far East in the ironclad *Ocean*, Fisher returned to the gunnery school at Portsmouth where he was again assigned to the torpedo branch. He became the first head of the new school devoted to instruction and experimental work in this important developing field in naval weaponry.

His next appointment at sea was in the Mediterranean, and after that he was promoted to captain of the ironclad *Bellerophon*, flagship of the North American and West Indies Station. For a short time he was posted to the

Plate 32.

HMS *Renown* and USS *New York*
Grassy Bay, Bermuda, 1898

During the Spanish-American War the U.S. fleet destroyed a Spanish squadron at the Battle of Santiago Bay, Cuba, on 3 July 1898. Admiral John Fisher, who had the Royal Navy command in Bermuda at the time, invited the American fleet to call at the island on its way back to New York.

The commander of the U.S. fleet, Admiral Sampson, flew his flag in the armored cruiser USS *New York*, which can be seen on the left of the picture.

The British flagship HMS *Renown* is in the center. She is flying a host of signal flags. At the top of the mainmast is her recognition signal (code letters GTKN), and below that: "Welcome to the United States Navy." On the foremast she is wearing the Vice-Admiral's flag and below it the instructions: "The visiting ships should stand-by to turn together to starboard, not in line ahead, and take-up mooring buoys. Further signals will be made by semaphore."

To the right of *Renown* can be seen the floating dock *Bermuda* which was stationed there for over forty years; its remains can still be seen stranded at Spaniard's Point.

In the background are the landward fortifications of Ireland Island and the splendid stone-built East Storehouse with its twin clock towers. A great pair of sheerlegs stands on the quayside before the storehouse. On the right are high coral cliffs surmounted by the seaward fortifications, and above them the Commissioner's House.

Sampson was Fisher's guest at a celebration banquet. Fisher proposed a toast to the President and people of the U.S.A. and their victory over the Spanish, but Sampson, a reticent man, had to be prompted by his flag captain to reply. When he eventually rose to his feet, his words were: "It must have been a damn fine old hen which laid the egg that hatched the American Eagle."

Mediterranean in command of a corvette called *Pallas* (calling to mind the ship of another generation commanded by Lord Cochrane). Once again he was sent as flag captain to the North American squadron, this time in the armored cruising ship *Northampton*. Fisher's cavalier behavior frequently caused resentment, but this often turned to respect after a longer period of association.

At the end of his second tour of duty in Bermuda he gained his first independent command; this was no less than the latest, the largest, and most powerful battleship, HMS *Inflexible*. She was a warship of technological importance, armed with enormous guns, and carrying the heaviest protection ever taken to sea. *Inflexible*'s hull was so broad in the beam to sustain this deadweight that her length exceeded her breadth by a ratio of only 4.5 to 1. She was the first with electric lighting and ventilation and the first with anti-roll tanks to maintain stability.

Inflexible happened to be assigned as guard ship to Villefranche during the period that Queen Victoria was spending a holiday at nearby Mentone. This brought Captain Fisher to the attention of Her Majesty. He managed to charm this notoriously formidable lady, and he revealed an unerring sense of just how far it was possible to go before polite facetiousness crossed the delicate border line into unforgivable disrespect.

In the following year *Inflexible* took part with the rest of the Mediterranean fleet in the bombardment of Alexandria. After a foray ashore which earned him some notoriety he was invalided home with dysentery, and his next appointment was in command of the gunnery school at Portsmouth. There his zeal for efficiency and the reform of antiquated practices was matched by his assertiveness, his penchant for outrageous generalizations, and by an increasing tendency towards autocratic behavior. At this time he began to cultivate associations with friends in high places, with newspapermen and politicians whom he would use to further his plans for naval reform.

In a similar manner to Cochrane, Fisher tended to accumulate enemies even as he forged new alliances and gained the support of those whom he impressed.

His next appointment was as Director of Naval Ordnance, where he regained for the Navy control over the design and supply of naval guns, which had hitherto been under the general direction of the Army. During Fisher's period of control strides were made in the development of quick-firing guns. The threat of torpedo-boat attack on battleships led to the production of a 4.7-inch caliber gun with integral cartridge and shell, capable of firing at the unprecedented rate of twelve rounds a minute. The Whitehead torpedo was improved so that it could travel at thirty knots and deliver a charge of 200 pounds. The pace of work in the Royal Dockyards quickened under his impatient intervention, resulting in much shorter construction times for new classes of warship.

In 1892 Fisher was appointed to the Board of Admiralty as Third Sea Lord, in which post he became responsible for all aspects of matériel for the Navy. Here he was closely involved with political decisions leading to a greatly increased program of warship construction. Fisher was in office at the time when the prodigious cruisers *Powerful* and *Terrible* were conceived to meet the prospect of Russian and French commerce raiders. He became closely identified with the development of improved torpedo craft, the invention of the torpedo-boat destroyer, and the introduction of submarines. He was created a Knight of the Bath in 1894.

Bermuda was Sir John Fisher's next appointment, this time as Commander in Chief. His flagship was HMS *Renown*, a smaller, lighter, and faster version of the battleships which formed the first line of the home fleet. She had been designed largely in response to his own particular ideas.

From the North America Station he was promoted to the Royal Navy's premier sea command, the Mediterranean Fleet. Before hoisting his flag in the Mediterranean he was sent by the Prime Minister, Lord Salisbury, to be Britain's naval delegate at The Hague Peace Conference of 1899. The government was not prepared to make any compromise on what was necessary to maintain supremacy at sea, and it looked to Fisher to impress on delegates

Britain's readiness to support diplomacy with force. "The supremacy of the British Navy," he wrote, "is the best security for the peace of the world."

Fisher then took charge in the Mediterranean like a whirlwind. Everything had to be done on the double. Cruises to foreign ports were conducted at full speed, protocol was slashed, and night maneuvers were conducted without navigation lights. To his wife he wrote: "We had only two collisions between torpedo boats which was wonderful, considering . . . it was all most exciting and as near to war conditions as it could be." There was emphasis on alertness and efficiency, and it was torpedo tactics that received the most attention. The range of gunnery practice was increased from 3,000 to 7,000 yards.

The office of First Lord of the Admiralty was a political appointment, filled by a member of the government of the day, and like all ministers he had to be a member of Parliament. The Sea Lords were serving naval officers, the First Sea Lord being the most senior professional post in the Navy.

In 1900 Lord Salisbury's Conservative government appointed Lord Selborne as First Lord, beginning a long and fruitful association with the fiery Fisher. Selborne invited the C-in-C of the Mediterranean Fleet to write to him personally with his views. Fisher did not hesitate, nor was he one to mince his words. With customary intemperance he asserted that the fleet was "criminally deficient in cruisers" and its position in the Mediterranean was "dangerous and serious."

He did not stop there. Incautiously, he wrote to newspapermen, inspiring press leaks which became more and more exasperating to his seniors at the Admiralty.

When Fisher transferred his flag from the North America Station to the Mediterranean his flagship went with him. Against all precedent he managed to get his favorite battleship reassigned to his new command.

But during the time that he was based in Malta he first began to develop his ideas for a new type of premier warship, one that would cap the crescendo of international competition in design. Fisher's vision was of a fighting ship

so much larger and more powerful that it would be able to overwhelm all other vessels.

Inevitably such a ship would be far more costly than existing ones. Inevitably there would be resistance within the world's largest navy to introducing a type which would render all existing battleships second-rate. Inevitably the military logic was that the nation that lacked the very best would face the prospect of being overcome piecemeal, regardless of numerical superiority. It was characteristic of the man that he spared no effort in forging his vision into reality.

The technical background was ripe for design revolution at the end of a period of evolutionary change. If the tactical object was to deliver concentrated firepower at the optimum location, superior armament and speed would provide the means. Improved propellants, guns, range finders, and fire control meant that the range of engagement had leapt for heavy guns; consequently guns of medium and smaller calibers would play no part in the initial action.

In a naval battle, much more than in a conflict on land, the first strike is generally crucial. Any disablement is likely to curb a ship's speed, seaworthiness, or fighting power. A minor deficiency leads to progressive inferiority: "To him that hath shall more be given, and to him that hath not shall be taken away even that which he had."

Finding the range and scoring the first hits were therefore the prime objectives, and for this purpose one needed to fire salvos, not broadsides. In this way aim could be corrected at intervals between the time taken to reload the guns. Conventional ships with four heavy guns were limited to two-gun salvos. Ships armed with eight or ten heavy guns would have an overwhelming advantage in quickly finding the range and then smothering the enemy with superior weight of fire.

There was a mathematical logic behind the concept of the all-big-gun ship, but Fisher's vision of HMS *Untouchable* went further. He dwelt on speed, so that the new ships could outstrip the enemy, head him off, and focus maximum firepower on one adversary at a time. The evenly matched set-piece battle, each ship engaging its opposite number, had no place in Fisher's plan. His fleet was expected to sweep across the bows of the enemy, bringing all guns to bear on the head of the opposing battle line.

At Malta the admiral found a receptive technical collaborator in William Gard, Chief Constructor at the Dockyard. They were not alone in pursuing this line of thought. For one, the Italian naval architect Vittorio Cuniberti published an authoritative article in 1903 advocating the all-big-gun ship.

In June 1902 Fisher was promoted to full Admiral and given the appointment of Second Sea Lord. In this post he took responsibility for matters of personnel.

The main achievement of these years had to do with entry and training, with the amalgamation of the technical branches of the Navy into the mainstream for promotion, and with reform of the conditions of service. Fisher continued to cultivate powerful connections through his annual vacations at the fashionable spa of Marienbad, and with the accession of King Edward VII he gained a priceless ally on the throne. Visits to Sandringham House and Balmoral Castle became features of his life.

His next appointment was as Port Admiral at Portsmouth. Once again his foresight was engaged by an emerging new weapon of naval warfare—the submarine. The first practicable and successful torpedo-carrying submarine had been developed by John Holland and adopted by the U.S. Navy. Arrangements had been made for submarine construction in Britain under exclusive license and Fisher seized on this development with enthusiasm.

In 1903 he supervised the first submarine flotilla exercises in the Solent, and he wrote that this new type of warship would revolutionize naval warfare, affecting the very roots of the country's defense. He foretold unrestricted submarine warfare against merchant ships, and he foresaw the invisible threat created by the mere possibility of the presence of submarines. Characteristically he took the Prince of Wales down in one of the early boats in the face of widespread criticism of the risk.

Towards the end of 1904 Fisher achieved the pinnacle of his profession, appointment to the office of First Sea Lord. He plunged into the stormiest passage of his career. Fisher recognized earlier than most the overt challenge to British supremacy on the seas which had been rapidly mounted in Germany under the stimulus of Grand Admiral Alfred von Tirpitz.

The change in the wind came abruptly. By that fall attitudes had been struck and policies had been adopted which were to lead inexorably to the outbreak of war in 1914. Many factors and many personalities came together in an aimless but sinister combination to bring about the catastrophe, and one of the salient features was the naval arms race between Germany and Britain.

Tirpitz and Fisher were the leading protagonists. In 1898 Tirpitz had initiated the construction of a great modern fleet. The navy law which he secured in that year provided for the building of a deepwater navy by a nation which already had the reputation of being the foremost military power in Europe. In British eyes the provocation was unmistakable: to Germany a fleet was a luxury, an inessential adornment to a powerful and self-sufficient nation. To England, her fleet was a matter of sheer survival.

Fisher went straight to the point. For five years he strained every fiber to meet the challenge being mounted from across the North Sea. It was in no small measure due to his energies that the Royal Navy was in condition to secure the country from invasion in 1914, to repulse the sally launched by the German fleet in April 1916, and to maintain the blockade which was, perhaps, the principal instrument in bringing about disintegration of the Kaiser's regime in October 1918.

The steps in the process are individually less important than the whole thrust of policy. Fisher had been impressed by the effect of underwater weapons—mine and torpedo—in the early stages of the Russo-Japanese War. He noted the annihilation of the Russians at Tsushima by a smaller but faster and more aggressively handled Japanese fleet. He presided over the conception and launch of his

Plate 33.

HMS *Dreadnought*
Port of Spain, Trinidad, 1906

The most famous battleship ever built was called *Dreadnought*, for she gave her name to those that followed after. First with an armament composed exclusively of long-range guns, and first to be powered by steam turbines, she was so much ahead of the competition that subsequent ships with equal characteristics were all distinguished by the term "dreadnought."

As with all new technology, success was uncertain. No one knew how a ship would act when eight twelve-inch guns were fired at once, and no one had tried steam turbines in a ship of this size before. Therefore the Navy decided to conduct *Dreadnought*'s sea trials far from what might become embarrassing observation.

The new ship was sent first to the Mediterranean. While passing through the Straits of Bonifacio, between Corsica and Sardinia, the steering gear jammed and the 18,000-ton ship helplessly performed circles before she was brought under control. The fault had no particular relationship with untried aspects of her design, but subsequent trials were con-

ducted in the West Indies for greater privacy. In all other respects, the new design of battleship proved an unqualified success.

The painting shows *Dreadnought* at moorings off Port of Spain, Trinidad, the coaling station where she replenished her bunkers for the homeward voyage. In the foreground one of the battleship's smart steam pinnaces is carrying officers to rejoin the ship, and on the left is the counter stern of a typical passenger liner of the period. *Dreadnought* is surrounded by lighters which are discharging coal, and steam is already being raised in preparation for going to sea.

Plate 34.

HMY *Victoria and Albert* and *Standart*

at Reval, Russia, 1908

In June 1908, King Edward VII paid a state visit to Russia in the Royal Yacht *Victoria and Albert*. Czar Nicholas II greeted him on board the Russian Imperial Yacht *Standart* anchored off the port of Reval at the mouth of the Gulf of Finland. Reval is the old name for what is now the city of Tallinn in Estonia.

The King was accompanied by his beautiful Queen Alexandra, the British Ambassador, and Sir John Fisher, the First Sea Lord. The British Royal Yacht was escorted by four German destroyers, which had been assigned by Prince Henry of Prussia to accompany her through the Baltic. On her passage through the Kiel Canal the *Victoria and Albert* had been escorted by a troop of Prussian cavalry.

Anchored alongside the *Standart* at Reval was the second Russian Imperial yacht, *Polarnaia-Sviezda*, wearing the flag of the Dowager Empress Marie, who was a sister of Queen Alexandra.

The Russian battleship *Slava* was guard ship for the occasion; she can be seen on the left of the picture.

The *Victoria and Albert* is flying her recognition signal GVKH in addition to the five flags worn by a Royal Yacht when she has the Sovereign on board. These are the Union flag at the jackstaff, the Admiralty flag at the fore, the Royal Standard at the main, the Union flag (for an Admiral of the Fleet) at the mizzen, and the White Ensign at the ensign staff.

The *Standart* is flying the Imperial Standard, the flags of an Admiral and of the Minister of Marine.

favorite project, the all-big-gun and turbine-powered battleship *Dreadnought*. He inspired the birth of the destroyer and of the battle cruiser. He backed the introduction of wireless, gunnery control, very large caliber guns, watertube boilers, and the conversion to oil fuel in place of coal. He advocated the use of mine barrages and of submarine warfare.

Fisher was in charge when British policy swung towards an alliance with the French. He pushed forward naval collaboration, pressing France to take the lead in the Mediterranean in order to free the main strength of the Royal Navy for concentration in the North Sea. He recalled weak ships from distant stations, pruned the fleet, groomed future leaders, and focused young officers' attention on the vital aspects of training for war.

Above all he battled in the corridors of power to secure funds to meet the mounting needs of the Navy. Year by year German expenditures on armaments climbed, and year by year British naval estimates were augmented to provide dreadnoughts to outnumber those in the German fleet.

As he grew old, Fisher became more and more preoccupied with personalities. He tended to see everything in extremes, and his views were never expressed in any but capital letters.

In 1908 the First Sea Lord accompanied the King on a state visit to Russia. The Czar received them in the Imperial Yacht off the port of Reval in the Baltic. The visit went far to consolidate relations with France's ally, although the British government clung to the principle of making no commitment which would oblige it to take part, in the event of a European war.

Fisher's administration was subjected to a final campaign inspired by his most prominent and bitter critic, Admiral Lord Beresford. A committee entrusted with investigating allegations of mismanagement handsomely vindicated the Board of Admiralty, but Fisher decided that the time had come for him to retire. He was honored with a peerage, and for his motto Lord Fisher chose "Fear God and Dread Nought."

There remained one further episode. In November 1914 Fisher was called back to the office of First Sea Lord. The First Lord of the Admiralty was a brash young Liberal politician called Winston Churchill. Things were not going well with the war at sea, and Churchill perceived Fisher as the man with the reputation, the vigor, and the imagination demanded by the situation.

The two men were in many ways kindred spirits. Together they schemed to dispatch battle cruisers to the Falklands in order to nail the commerce raiders of Graf von Spee. The stroke was brilliantly successful.

At first things went swimmingly, but before long the two men fell out. Fisher's judgment had become warped by age and conceit. His vision stretched too far ahead, encompassing the dominance of air power and amphibious operations with motorized landing craft, concepts that were to become reality only after thirty years. Churchill became mired in controversy as a result of the Navy's failure to force a passage through the Dardanelles.

Interestingly, Fisher's proposal for making landings on the Baltic coast of Germany bears some resemblance to Cochrane's strategic thinking for the war against Napoleon. Neither man carried the weight of service opinion with him.

Within seven months of resuming office Fisher resigned. Churchill, too, was driven from office when the ineffectual Gallipoli campaign gradually took on the dimensions of a disaster.

There was a sorry postscript to Fisher's career. On account of his prestige he was pressed by a number of important figures to remain in office. He proposed terms which would have given him dictatorial power. His offer was contemptuously dismissed, and when victory was finally achieved in World War I, Fisher failed to receive the national recognition which was his due.

Lord Fisher died in 1920, and no memorial was ever erected to commemorate his career of public service.

Plate 35.

HMS *Terrible*
Hurd's Channel, Bermuda, 1852

The principal approach through the surrounding coral reef to the island of Bermuda is at the northeast extremity. Hurd's Channel, now known as The Narrows, provides a passage from the open ocean to the sheltered water of Murray's Anchorage, passing very close to the shore. Fort St. Catherine, constructed on the headland at this point, formed a most effective defense.

Sailing ships trying to negotiate this narrow, doglegged channel were entirely at the mercy of cannon mounted on the stone fortifications, but steamships were not quite so helpless.

HMS *Terrible* was a paddle frigate built in 1842-1845. She was the largest paddle warship ever built and mounted two decks of guns, four 68-pounders and four 56-pounders on each, plus three smaller guns. She had a top speed of about fifteen knots. After serving in the Black Sea during the Crimean War, in 1869 she took part in towing the floating dock from England to Bermuda. *Terrible* acted as the rudder while the dock was being towed by two big ironclads.

The frigate is "making her number" as she passes the fort, and at the mizzen she is wearing the broad red pendant of a Commodore. The Union flag was worn at the fore when entering or leaving a British port.

BERMUDA

Bermuda is a speck of land surrounded by a seemingly endless expanse of water. On the same latitude as Charleston, South Carolina, it is 1,000 miles equally from Antigua, Cuba, Florida, and Nova Scotia.

To stay there is like being on board ship: one is constantly made aware of the changing moods of the sea and sky. There is a perpetual sea breeze, damp and cool, which masks the burning quality of the sun. Turquoise water shades to ultramarine, then to indigo towards the horizon. The island is twenty miles long but at no point is it more than a mile and a half wide. From most places one can see the sea; often it is visible on both sides at the same time. Graceful long-tailed seabirds are never far off, wheeling endlessly over the cliffs.

Bermuda is a coral island, a long, curved sliver of land shaped like a scorpion. To the north, up to fifteen miles of coral reef separate the island from the ocean deep. Few indeed are the channels by which ships can approach. The main one is at the eastern extremity; this is where vessels from Europe first penetrated and it is still the only access for ships of any size. From there they must negotiate one of two buoyed channels, picking their way carefully within the reef around to the western end of Bermuda where lies the entrance to the Great Sound, to Hamilton Harbour, and to the naval dockyard at the scorpion's tail.

From the time of its discovery early in the sixteenth century sailors who visited Bermuda did so by accident: all were victims of shipwreck. In 1604 a squadron carrying colonists to Virginia became scattered in a storm and the flagship was wrecked on the reef. The castaways, which included the governor-designate, managed to get ashore where they built a new ship in which to complete their journey. Two of the company chose to stay behind, and they became the first residents of Bermuda.

The island was at that time forested with cedars, which provided good timber for boatbuilding. This has led over the years to a great tradition of boat design and construction, made famous by the innovation of Bermuda Rig. Island sportsmen evolved generations of racing boats known as Bermuda Fitted Dinghies.

The year-round climate of Bermuda is steadied by the great mass of the surrounding ocean. No one who has visited this enchanting island can fail to have been seduced by the flowering trees. Blazing scarlet flamboyants are the most gorgeous, but they include silver-green oleanders covered with pale pink flowers, the delicate lemon yellow cascade of laburnum, brilliant individual blossoms of hibiscus, scented frangipani, feathery casuarinas, and rattling palms. The birds, too, are something special. Bermuda longtails bear an aspect of fantasy which is entirely appropriate to their delightful habitat: they are to be found nowhere else in the world.

The island is not on the direct path of sailing vessels following the Northeast Trade Winds on passage from Europe to the Caribbean, nor of coastwise traffic from there to the eastern seaboard of North America. It lies to the south of the track of ships making use of the Westerlies on the return voyage to Europe. Bermuda became significant, nevertheless, on account of its strategic location and because ships based there could intercept trade on all these routes.

By the middle of the eighteenth century the islands of the Caribbean had assumed an importance in the eyes of European nations which is difficult to appreciate in the twentieth. The sugar industry of the West Indies was the largest economic enterprise the world had known, and the commerce in sugar, molasses, rum, cotton, tobacco, cinnamon, and mace was a major element in worldwide trade.

Britain, France, Holland, and Spain vied with one another for possession of the most prized of the West Indies. At the end of the Seven Years' War Britain returned the captured island of Martinique to France in favor of retaining Canada, but there were many in England who thought the country had made the wrong choice.

The extinction of French power in North America, however, presaged the revolt of thirteen of the British colonies, and their success in the Revolutionary War deprived Britain of port facilities in the continental seaboard between Kingston, Jamaica, and Halifax, Nova Scotia.

Bermuda suddenly acquired a new importance. The Royal Navy sent a surveyor to the island who sounded out two deepwater anchorages within the reef, and by 1800 a naval station was established at St. George's, at the east end of the main island.

Although wooden sailing ships were less dependent on shore bases than their successors, facilities were required nevertheless for "careening." This operation consisted of tilting a ship to one side in order to expose half the hull at a time to allow it to be scraped clean of marine growth. Fouling of the bottom would reduce a ship's speed and it also fostered attack by teredo worm. Shore depots were needed for replenishment of stores and, most important, of powder and shot.

St. George's afforded a sheltered anchorage for "carenage," and a stone warehouse for munitions was built on the waterfront. In 1810 the Navy decided to build

dockyard facilities. The site chosen was Ireland Island, which forms the western extremity of Bermuda. It is remote from the channel which provides access through the reef at the eastern end of the island complex, but its seaward and its landward approaches are more easily defensible than those of St. George's. The deepwater anchorage of Grassy Bay is enclosed by Ireland Island.

As the Navy entered the age of steam Bermuda, and other overseas bases like it, assumed greater importance. Steamers were uneconomical in the early days, therefore endurance was limited and widespread coaling stations became strategically desirable. The best steam coal was shipped from Cardiff and stockpiled for naval use. Steam engines required repair and maintenance, and the hulls of iron ships needed scraping and scrubbing more urgently than the copper-sheathed bottoms of wooden ships.

Ingress and egress through The Narrows, that tricky dogleg passage that gives access through the perimeter of the reef, is far less difficult for steamers than for sailing ships, and operations became less constrained by the broad pattern of the prevailing winds. With its commanding position at the center of the western part of the North Atlantic the island provided a secure strategic base equally accessible to the North American seaboard, the Bahamas, the Greater and Lesser Antilles, and to the Gulf and Caribbean coasts of Central and South America.

When the United States tried to take possession of Canada in the War of 1812, a retaliatory expedition into the Chesapeake Bay region was mounted from the base in Bermuda. Thereafter the prospect of an American attempt to capture the island was real enough to call for extensive measures of fortification. Many of the land defenses, including the impressive fortress on a hilltop commanding the eastern side of the capital, Hamilton, were built on the recommendation of a commission headed by the Duke of Wellington. Some of the fort's massive rifled muzzle-loading guns can still be seen, although the gun carriages which could elevate them above the ramparts for firing and then lower them out of sight for reloading have not survived.

During the American Civil War, St. George's

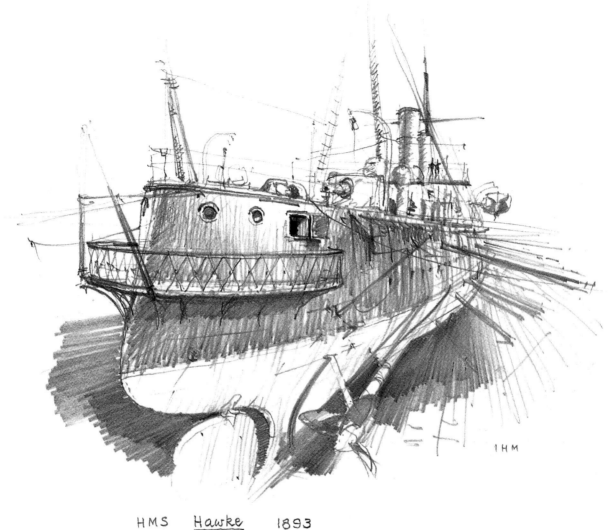

HMS Hawke 1893

became a hotbed of Confederate agents, and Bermudians grew fat on the proceeds of running cargoes through the Union blockade. In anticipation of an attempt at invasion a powerful British squadron was dispatched for defense of the island. In addition to oceangoing ships there was an inshore squadron which included the Crimean War armored battery HMS *Terror*.

Following the Southern defeat, the coastal defense squadron was enhanced by the ironclad ram HMS *Scorpion*, which had been under construction in England for the Confederate government when she was seized to prevent delivery. A strong defensive line of earthworks including emplacements for heavy guns was thrown across the landward approach to the naval base on Ireland Island. These fortifications can still be seen.

In the early twentieth century the island's defenses were once again brought up to date, and the coastal batteries were equipped with breech-loading 9.2-inch guns. The main protection against raiders, nevertheless, remained the difficulty of finding the passage through the coral reef. Within recent years a Russian cruise ship, scorning the use of local pilots, came to grief on the rocks.

Plate 36.

HMS *Northampton*
Bermuda, 1880

Jackie Fisher was posted to HMS *Northampton* as captain in 1879. The ironclad was the flagship of Vice Admiral Sir L.F. M'Clinton.

The iron floating-dock *Bermuda*, in the foreground, was installed at Grassy Bay in 1869 and remained in service until 1902.

Northampton was an armored cruising ship, built in response to the construction by Russia of armored cruisers. Intended for service on distant stations, she was sent first to the West Indies, but at thirteen knots she was too slow to be of good use as a cruiser. She was armed with four ten-inch rifles, eight nine-inch rifles, and six smaller guns, and she carried two sixty-foot torpedo boats. Her armor was a combination of the usual side belt with protective decks at bow and stern. The four heavier guns were placed in diagonal corners of the main deck battery, firing through embrasures and able to traverse through wide arcs of fire.

In the background is Ireland Island dockyard, the East Storehouse being prominent with twin clock towers.

The most important facility in the dockyard was the floating dock. Inspection, cleaning, or repair of a metal hull requires that the ship be berthed in dry dock. In Bermuda it was found that the limestone was insufficiently impervious to enable the excavation of a conventional dry dock, and so a floating dock was built of iron. This dock, the largest in the world, was built on the Thames and towed to Bermuda in 1869. One of two ironclads which shared the job was HMS *Warrior*.

The remains of the original Bermuda dock can still be seen if one goes swimming at Spaniard's Point. It was replaced in service in 1906 by a new dock, again the world's largest, and the old one was bought by a German firm for scrapping. The partly dismantled dock eventually broke loose and was beached: it is said that the new owners were more interested in charting the passage through the coral reef than in recovering their acquisition.

Over a period of 160 years the Royal Navy posted eighty-four officers to Bermuda as Commander in Chief. The command was described as the North America and West Indies Station, and it included the region from British Guiana to the St. Lawrence, including a second naval base at Halifax.

One of the admirals installed at Bermuda was Thomas Cochrane, who was sent there in 1848 as the Earl of Dundonald. This was during the last decade of the long mastery of sail. Another was Sir John Fisher. He took over the command in 1897 at a moment when the ironclad was at the very pinnacle of its power and reputation.

In the course of two world wars Bermuda served as a base for operations to protect merchant shipping from German raiders and submarines. Its main importance was as a communications center, as a mustering point for convoys, and in the Second World War as an aircraft base and staging post. It was one of the military bases leased by Britain to the United States in 1940, and remains to this day a U.S. Naval Air Station.

In the 1930s Pan American Airways and Imperial Airways jointly started a passenger flying-boat service from Bermuda to New York: in those days Europe was beyond the

regular operational range of aircraft. Two well-known liners, *Monarch of Bermuda* and *Queen of Bermuda*, brought the great majority of tourists to the island. Each ship had a gray hull, white upperworks, and three red funnels capped in black; they looked like miniature versions of the great Cunarder *Queen Mary*.

Today tourists arrive in far greater numbers by jet, but Hamilton is still a popular destination for cruises. A fine maritime museum now occupies the substantial powder magazine of the old R.N. Dockyard on Ireland Island.

Plate 37.

HMS *Illustrious*
Grand Harbour, Malta, 1898

A squadron of the Royal Navy's latest battleships moored bow to stern in Grand Harbour in 1898. The leading ship is HMS *Illustrious* of the *Majestic* class; astern of her lie her sister ships HMS *Caesar* and *Hannibal* and the protected cruiser *Hawke*. To the left is the battleship *Empress of India* of the *Royal Sovereign* class and beyond is the cruiser *Theseus*.

The warships all face the harbor mouth, ready at immediate notice to slip their moorings and stand out to sea. This was towards the close of the era when a force of ironclads based in the island of Malta held the balance of power in the Inland Sea and exerted leverage in the politics of southern Europe, North Africa, and the Levant.

Illustrious served for six years in the Mediterranean, where she took part in the international operation to suppress insurrection in Crete in 1898. Subsequently she saw service at sea in home waters until 1912, and thereafter as guard ship at various ports until her retirement in 1920.

The *Majestic* class was the culmination of Victorian warship design. Designed by Sir William White, they had a high freeboard and provided a steady gun platform well clear of interference from heavy seas.

The main armament consisted of four twelve-inch guns of wire-wound construction, newly developed by Armstrong. The guns used smokeless powder, which was slower burning than older type powder, making possible the use of longer barrels to obtain higher muzzle velocity and therefore greater range, accuracy, and penetrating power. The ships were the first to be equipped with telescopic gunsights.

MALTA

The last stop on our journey through the era of the ironclads is Malta. Nowhere in the world can one more readily detect the whiff of their coal smoke.

Like Bermuda, Malta owed its importance to its strategic location, to the existence of a fine deepwater anchorage, and the fact that the whole island was small enough that it needed no large army for its defense.

Malta consists of a limestone outcrop midway between Europe and Africa. It lies some sixty miles off the southern coast of Sicily, in the center of the channel which links the basins of the western and eastern Mediterranean. There are two main islands, Malta itself, which is seventeen miles by nine, and the smaller neighboring island of Gozo.

In pre-history, Malta was used as a stepping-stone by early man en route between the continents, and since the early days of navigation it has been a port of refuge on the passage from east to west. The Phoenicians first found Malta to be a valuable base, and after them the island became a possession successively of Carthage, Rome, and Byzantium, of Arabs, Sicilian Normans, and then of the Kingdom of Spain. The people of the island form a distinct ethnic and cultural unit, clearly different from Italians and from any other mainland group.

It was in 1530 that the Knights of St. John arrived in Malta. The last organized group in succession to the Crusaders, the Christian knights had been evicted by Islamic Turks from their stronghold of Rhodes, an island close to the Turkish coast.

The knights made their headquarters overlooking a spectacular harbor on the east coast of Malta. Grand Harbour is an extraordinary topographical formation, comprising a deep inlet of the sea elaborated with numerous creeks. A second inlet called Marsamxett lies half a mile to the north, and pinched between the two is a rocky spine straddled by the modern city of Valletta. Cliffs surrounding the inlets drop abruptly into deep water, and the harbor of Valletta affords secure moorings for a fleet of oceangoing ships.

The Knights of St. John found a base for their oared galleys on the south side of Grand Harbour. They built their stronghold of St. Angelo on a narrow promontory, and they fortified the seaward cliffs on both sides of the entrance to the harbor.

Thirty-five years after they arrived in Malta, the knights were pursued by Islam. Malta lay in the path of Islamic expansion to the west, and a force of 35,000 men with siege artillery was landed by the Turkish fleet in 1565. The knights themselves numbered 600, supported by some 7,000 auxiliary troops, but they fought the invaders with legendary heroism.

The Venetians who were later besieged by the Turks in Crete held out for twenty-four years, but the Great Siege of Malta lasted only for a ferocious four months. The contest was unbelievably bitter. The Turks lost their leader, the notorious Dragut, during the capture of Fort St. Elmo. In fury they tied the dead bodies of the defenders to wooden crosses and floated them up the harbor past Fort St. Angelo. The surviving knights under Grand Master de la Valette

F. S. Jauréguiberry   1897

responded by loading their cannons with the heads of Turkish prisoners. The battle was so bloody that the Turks lost two out of every three men in the whole army. When the forces of Islam finally gave up, the Christian knights had been reduced to half their original number.

The searing experience of this clash between the religions of east and west left its mark on Malta. Nowhere in the modern world can be found a community more devout.

The victorious knights set about building a new capital, which they named Valletta, and they employed the foremost Italian military engineers to design impregnable fortifications. The Cathedral and the Palace of the Grand Master occupy the ridge of the spine, and the Auberges of the various Langues (national detachments), were built within the confines of the walls. Sandstone cliffs were carved into the required geometry, and ramparts formed of quarried stone were built to merge imperceptibly into the underlying rock. The whole city seems to be formed of one material, a pale honey-colored stone.

The island of Malta presents a harmonious land-scape, the towns and villages echoing the golden design of Valletta. Cupolas float above each community, country roads are bordered by dykes of the same material, and blank ends of houses crowd close on both sides of village streets. The scent of orange blossom wafts over a wall, and a narrow grille suggests the existence of a secret garden.

The island lies bare in summer. Fields are defined by walls, there is a single miniature forest of trees, and the island has no perennial rivers. Malta is not always a place of scorching heat; in early spring it is a paradise of wildflowers. The sea is pewter gray, the cliffs are more creamy than gold, and the miniature orchids are a haze of violet. The companion island of Gozo appears only faintly in the mist across the narrow stretch of the Comino Channel.

The Knights of St. John remained undisturbed in possession of their kingdom until 1798. That year the rocky island took on a new strategic importance, as Napoleon Bonaparte led a military expedition from Toulon to land in Egypt, bent on creating a French empire stretching overland to India.

Britain was fighting tenaciously in the long-drawn war to prevent French domination, and the Royal Navy had imposed a blockade on Toulon as well as on French Channel and Atlantic ports. Admiral Nelson's fleet was blown off station in a gale, enabling 500 ships of Napoleon's force to stand out to sea and disappear.

The hunt for that fleet went on for two and a half months. Nelson finally found the French anchored in Aboukir Bay at the mouth of the Nile in Egypt, the general and his army having long since gone ashore. The British ships bore down at dusk and some of them managed to pass inshore of the French line. Converging on both sides of the Frenchmen, the British men-of-war captured or destroyed one ship after the other. In an age when sea battles were very rarely conclusive the Battle of the Nile, which ended in the annihilation of the French fleet, was unprecedented.

During the voyage to Egypt Napoleon had landed and taken possession of Malta, leaving a small garrison. Only two French line-of-battle ships survived the Battle of the Nile, and after their escape they headed back to the island. Napoleon himself slipped home in a frigate, but the army was left to its fate.

In Malta the French quickly made themselves unpopular. Within a few months the populace rose in revolt, and the French garrison was obliged to take refuge inside the fortifications of Valletta. British ships returning from Egypt put into Malta, and a blockade was imposed.

It took two years before the French garrison was forced to surrender. The leisurely siege was punctuated by rousing engagements between French relief squadrons sent from Toulon and the British ships enforcing the blockade. One night the *Guillaume Tell*, one of the French liners which had escaped from Egypt, sailed from Grand Harbour but was intercepted by a frigate. She put up such a spirited resistance that two British ships-of-the-line were mauled before she was dismasted and forced to strike her colors.

Once the French had been evicted from Malta a British expedition was sent to Egypt, which, in alliance with the Ottomans, defeated the French army left in that country and brought the overland route to India indisputably under British control.

In 1801 prolonged negotiations were started to bring the war to an end, and the future of the strategic island became the subject of particularly severe dispute. The Maltese sent a delegation to London appealing for Britain not to withdraw. The Treaty of Amiens was finally concluded early in 1802, under the terms of which France's prewar colonial possessions in the West Indies and in India were restored, but Britain declined to evacuate Malta.

The treaty brought only a short respite. In 1803 Napoleon, now in the role of First Consul, used the occupation of Malta as a pretext for reopening hostilities against Britain.

The victor of the Battle of the Nile was posted back to the Mediterranean. Admiral Lord Nelson made Malta his headquarters, and he wrote his appreciation that the island was not only an important outwork in the defense of India, but that it would also provide great influence in the Levant and in Southern Europe. "I hope we shall never give it up," he said.

The second phase of the Napoleonic Wars ended in 1814 with the abdication of the Emperor and the allied occupation of Paris. The peace treaty acknowledged British sovereignty over Malta, and this was again confirmed by the Congress of Vienna following Napoleon's ultimate defeat at Waterloo.

The presence of the British was welcomed by the people of the island. A genial atmosphere seems to have been generated by the Navy, and mutual respect prevailed

the Southern States. The island continues to supply flowers and vegetables to northern Europe from fields which were put under cultivation at this time. A railway line was built from Valletta to the northwest end of the main island, with a tunnel under the old hilltop capital of Mdina.

With the introduction of steamship services through the Red Sea to India, connecting with the overland link from Alexandria to Suez, traffic along the length of the Mediterranean became of increasing importance. In 1869 the Suez Canal was opened, and shipping from Europe to India and the Far East streamed through the Mediterranean. Malta assumed greater significance to Britain as the principal outpost on the "lifeline of the Empire."

Towards the end of the century it became evident that an enemy might not be prevented from landing in the northwest of the island, and that modern naval guns such as seventeen-inch rifles in the *Dandolo* and *Duilio* could outrange the coastal batteries. A new system of landward fortifications was built across the island and thirty-eight-ton guns, capable of keeping enemy armored ships at arm's length, were mounted in modern low-lying gun emplacements. These elaborate defense works were known as the Victoria Lines.

Grand Harbour in Valletta became a kind of stage setting. The menacing black ironclads would come gliding into the narrow waters, brasswork gleaming, flags snapping, white-helmeted Marines mustered under a taut canvas awning on the quarterdeck. The presence of the powerful ships was a deliberate display of naval capability.

As rivalry grew between Germany and Britain in the early years of the new century the importance of Malta declined. By 1914 the heavy metal had been concentrated in the North Sea.

Malta was used by the French and British in the First World War as a base for the Gallipoli campaign, and it became the support for operations to blockade the Austrian fleet in the Adriatic. In the last two years of the war submarine warfare became the chief activity, in the Mediterranean no less than in the Atlantic.

By the outbreak of the Second World War it had

throughout 163 years of British administration. The arrangement had obvious benefits for both parties.

Malta became the principal British overseas naval base and it fulfilled that role throughout the nineteenth century. A dockyard was established, complete with graving docks and all the necessary support facilities. A permanent army garrison was stationed in the island, and the defenses of Grand Harbour were further strengthened by the construction of a series of outlying forts and seaward-facing artillery batteries. At the middle of the century there were 330 coastal defense guns, including 68-pounder muzzle-loading rifles.

During the Crimean War Malta became the support base for operations in the Black Sea, and a large hospital was established at Bighi Bay. At the time of the American Civil War cotton was introduced to the island, the crop being exported to fill some of the gap left by the blockade of became obvious that air power would impose constraints on the use of surface ships, and it seemed that Malta would be untenable in such close proximity to hostile airfields in Sicily and North Africa. Nevertheless the island was not abandoned, even though the main part of the British fleet was transferred to Alexandria.

The Italian and German campaigns in North Africa were aimed at the capture of the Suez Canal and access to the oil fields of the Middle East. Supplies for the Axis armies were shipped from Italian ports to Libya. Submarines and aircraft based in Malta did enormous destruction to this traffic. They were joined by destroyers and light cruisers which, in spite of enemy air power, were able to operate at night. British forces based in Malta sank half a million tons of Italian shipping and twenty-one warships.

Air attacks on Malta commenced at the outbreak of war and continued almost daily for three years. The climax occurred in 1942, when 14,000 tons of bombs were dropped on the island. This compares with 250 tons of bombs dropped on the city of Coventry during the Blitz. In the same period 1,500 enemy aircraft were shot down over Malta.

No fighter squadrons were based on the island at the outbreak of war. It was discovered that the naval stores included crates containing the dismantled parts of three biplanes, Sea Gladiators for use on the aircraft carrier *Eagle*[1]. The obsolete fighter planes were assembled and for the first few months were the only aircraft able to take to the air in opposition to Italian bombers. The three planes became known to the Maltese as *Faith*, *Hope*, and *Charity*.

An Italian seaborne landing was repulsed, and German plans for an assault by paratroops and gliders were called off only at the very last minute. Two reconnaissance parties had already been landed before the operation was canceled, apparently as a result of Hitler's concern over heavy casualties sustained during the airborne invasion of Crete.

In Malta more than 1,100 civilians lost their lives in air raids (one and a half percent of the entire population was injured), and dreadful losses were sustained by mer-chant ships attempting to run supplies. In August 1942 a convoy arrived only in the nick of time to save the island from capitulation. Nine out of fourteen merchant ships were sunk, the rest all being damaged, and warship losses included a carrier, two cruisers, and a destroyer.

In April 1942 the King awarded the George Cross "to honour the brave people of Malta and to bear witness to a heroism and devotion that will long be famous." The national flag carries the cross in the upper left quarter.

On September 8, 1943, Italy withdrew from the war and under the terms of the armistice the Italian fleet steamed to Malta to surrender. On that date each year a service takes place in the Chapel of St. Anne in the fortress of St. Angelo to mark the anniversary of raising the Great Siege in 1565 and also to celebrate the end of the Battle of Malta.

In 1963 Malta became an independent country and in 1979 the Royal Navy severed its long connection with the island.

In the modern world Malta has ceased to have the same strategic importance, and, like Bermuda, the island has focused on tourism as a means of livelihood. Its dock-yard is now exclusively devoted to the repair of merchant shipping and a jazz festival takes place each June in the incomparable setting of Grand Harbour.

Like Venice, Valletta affords a marvelous subject for painting, just as it provided a theatrical backdrop for pageantry. There is no more fitting place to terminate an excursion through the world in which a handful of black ironclads commanded such authority that their mere presence kept the peace.

[1] This ship started as a battleship under construction in England for the Chilean Navy. Work stopped after the outbreak of war in 1914 and she was finally completed as an aircraft carrier in 1920. Her Chilean name was *Almirante Cochrane*.

Plate 38.

HMS *Camperdown*
Grand Harbour, Malta, 1894

James Morris, in the third volume of his trilogy on the British Empire, writes this of the Royal Navy at Malta: "Some capital ships were always based at Malta, for everyone to see, and their tremendous shapes were inescapable in Valletta, glimpsed at the end of city streets or basking in the sun, like sea-monsters, below the public gardens."

The year is 1894 and the ship in the foreground is HMS *Camperdown*, a long, black ironclad of the *Admiral* class. Two of her principal armament of 13.5-inch breech-loading rifled guns can be seen naked, mounted on top of the forecastle barbette. The after pair of guns is concealed by a canvas awning stretched over the quarterdeck.

In the background of this view from a terrace above the fortifications of Floriana are the waters of French Creek and the town of Senglea. Moored in the center, behind *Camperdown*, is the turret ship HMS *Nile*, and on the left and in the right background are two ships of the new *Royal Sovereign* class, HMS *Ramillies* and *Revenge*.

Warships of the era had tall masts supporting fighting tops equipped with light, quick-firing guns, delicate bridge-work spanning the superstructure fore and aft, many ships' boats perched on the upperworks, and large goose-necked ventilators leading to the stokeholds and engine rooms. Many battleships had twin funnels set side-by-side.

BIBLIOGRAPHY

Alden, John D. *The American Steel Navy*. Annapolis: Naval Institute Press, 1972.

Archibald, E.H.H. *The Fighting Ship of the Royal Navy*. Poole: Blandford Press, 1984.

Attard, Joseph. *The Battle of Malta*. London: William Kimber, 1980.

Bradford, Ernle. *The Great Siege*. London: 1958.

Brown, D.K. *Before the Ironclad*. London: Conway Maritime Press, 1990.

Cannery, Donald L. *The Old Steam Navy*. Annapolis: Naval Institute Press, 1990.

Elliott, Peter. *The Cross and the Ensign*. Cambridge: Patrick Stephens, 1980.

Gardiner, Robert, ed. *All the World's Fighting Ships 1860-1905*. London: Conway Maritime Press, 1979.

Gibbons, Tony. *The Complete Encyclopedia of Battleships and Battlecruisers*. London: Salamander Books, 1983.

Headrick, Daniel R. *The Tools of Empire*. New York: Oxford University Press, 1981.

Hough, Richard. *Admirals in Collision*. London: Hamish Hamilton, 1959.

____. *Dreadnought*. London: George Allen & Unwin, 1968.

____. *First Sea Lord*. London: George Allen & Unwin, 1969.

Jane, Fred T., ed. *Fighting Ships, 1914*. London: Sampson Low, Marston, 1914.

Keegan, John. *The Price of Admiralty*. London: Hutchinson, 1988.

Kemp, Peter. *The Oxford Companion to Ships and the Sea*. New York: Oxford University Press, 1976.

Lambert, Andrew. *Battleships in Transition*. London: Conway Maritime Press, 1984.

____. *Warrior*. London: Conway Maritime Press, 1987.

____. *The Last Sailing Battlefleet*. London: Conway Maritime Press, 1991.

Lloyd, Christopher. *Lord Cochrane*. London: Longmans, Green, 1947.

MacKay, Robert. *Fisher of Kilverstone*. Oxford: Clarendon Press, 1973.

Marder, Arthur J. *Fear God and Dread Nought*. London: Oxford University Press, 1952-1959.

Massie, Robert K. *Dreadnought*. New York: Random House, 1991.

Morris, James. *Pax Britannica*. London: Faber & Faber, 1968.

____. *Heaven's Command*. London: Faber & Faber, 1973.

____. *Farewell the Trumpets*. London: Faber & Faber, 1978.

Parkes, Oscar. *British Battleships*. London: Seeley Service, 1956.

Silverstone, Paul L. *Warships of the Civil War Navies*. Annapolis: Naval Institute Press, 1989.

Stranack, Ian. *The Andrew and the Onions*. Bermuda: Bermuda Maritime Museum Press, 1990.

Sutton, Jean. *Lords of the East*. London: Conway Maritime Press, 1981.

Thomas, Donald. *Cochrane*. London: Andre Deutsch, 1978.

Trotter, Wilfrid Pym. *The Royal Navy in Old Photographs*. London: J.M. Dent & Sons, 1975.

Wilson, Timothy. *Flags at Sea*. London: Her Majesty's Stationery Office, 1986.

INDEX

HMS Takaroa 1887

IHM